Zen Buddhism and the Reality of Suffering

"Dr Giraldi, who has done much research into stress and the effects and treatment of serious disease, here relates his experience to Buddhist teachings and, especially, to the practice of Zen. We all face the prospect of disease and death, and Dr Giraldi has found in this ancient wisdom and unique practice a key to peace of mind in the midst of so much suffering and trauma. He relates the history of the tradition and the personal story of his own involvement and explores the mysteries of the mind in its encounter with both its own hidden depths and the challenge of impermanence. This is thus a work of special interest to all of us concerned with the unity of body and mind and the passage of life and death."

—David Brazier is psychotherapist, authority on Buddhist psychology, author of *Zen Therapy* and many other books

"This important book engages with a meeting of two very different cultures that began over a century ago and continues in our time. During this period, both sides have learnt from each other, and each has been developing in its own right. Buddhists have learnt something about engaging with the world, and Western therapies have learnt something about disengaging.

Tullio Giraldi brings out the archipelago of realities that has resulted from this meeting. We are less inclined to see Freud or other Western gurus as offering universal truths but rather solutions that worked for them and some others. He makes clear that the challenge for each of us is to find our own way and outlines how Zen might help."

—David Healy is a former Professor of *Psychiatry at McMaster University in Canada* and at *Bangor and Cardiff Universities in the UK*, and *Founder of Data Based Medicine and RxISK.org*

Tullio Giraldi

Zen Buddhism and the Reality of Suffering

palgrave
macmillan

Tullio Giraldi
Department of Life Sciences
University of Trieste
Trieste, Italy

ISBN 978-3-031-69243-7 ISBN 978-3-031-69244-4 (eBook)
https://doi.org/10.1007/978-3-031-69244-4

This Palgrave Macmillan imprint is published by the registered company Springer Nature Switzerland AG.
The registered company address is: Gewerbestrasse 11, 6330 Cham, Switzerland

My activity could not have happened without the continued understanding and support of my family and particularly of my wife, with her loving patience and never-ending supply of coffee and delicious sweets prepared by her, a substantial assistance during my writing.

Acknowledgements

This book is the third of a trilogy which was written about Zen Buddhism and existential mental ailments mainly having in mind the many students that I encountered during my long professional life.

My activities began as an experimental pharmacologist, later involved into clinical pharmacological research. These experiences were accompanied by a deep interest into human nature and mind, which led me also to become a clinical psychologist, and psychotherapist as a transactional analyst. At the same time, these interests were deeply tied with the discovery and practice of Buddhism and Zen, which crowned somehow the research and clinical interest in mental disorders and existential sufferings and their management.

These activities were realised at my alma mater, the University of Trieste, Italy, and the other Universities and research institutions where I have been working and where I was a visiting scientist and researcher. A remarkable experience was additionally provided by my participation to the radical and revolutionary changes in psychiatric care of mental diseases which were realised in Trieste, Italy, from the 1980s through the work of Franco Basaglia.

An experience even more engaging was since the 1970s the practice of Rinzai Zen under the guide of Engaku Taino at the Monastery of Zenshinji Scaramuccia in the hills near Orvieto, Italy.

During my long career and the involvement into the interests which accompanied it, I had thus the opportunity of meeting a host of extraordinary personalities. This happened with colleagues engaged in the demandingly exact field of scientific research and with clinicians involved in the humane and respectful care of people with mental ailments. Even more compelling has been the accompanying practice of Zen, which provided a central reference encompassing all the particulars of the other experiences.

The constant contact with students and young professionals in training in these fields provided a similarly unique experience, not only for what I could give them but especially for the enrichment which I received from them.

It would be impossible to try to name all of them, but I am sure that they may recognise themselves even in these few lines and in the more details which are provided in the chapters of this book, and realise the great and sincere gratitude I owe to, and have for all of them.

My most sincere hope is that my students and colleagues, and all the interested readers, may find in this book a guide for orienting themselves in the challenging areas of existential ailments and of the way to escape the ensuing sufferings.

Introductory Note

Since this work is also intended for a general readership, the terms of Pali and Sanskrit origins are transliterated without the diacritical marks that would have been appropriate in a work of a more scholarly nature.

Similarly, the Japanese words will be used retaining the system of Romanization used in the original documents cited.

'Mindfulness' is the word which had been used as a translation of the Pali term *sati* since the early English translations of Buddhist scriptures. With the diffusion of the mindfulness movement and its applications in the West, particularly with its diffusion into the world of medicine and psychology, the terms mindfulness and mindfulness meditation have also been used in an undifferentiated way as a synonym of meditation. The terms of mindfulness and meditation will be therefore retained without further specification as used in the original documents cited.

Contents

About the Author

Tullio Giraldi is a full professor of pharmacology, now retired, at the University of Trieste, Italy. He is an Eminent Scholar at the Faculty of Medicine, where he taught pharmacological topics to under- and post-graduate students, and neuropsychopharmacology and clinical psychology at the Faculty of Psychology.

He was a visiting scientist in many foreign institutions and is currently a visiting professor at the King's College London, UK.

He has been ordained Rinzai Zen lay monk at Zenshin-ij Monastery, Italy, in the lineage of Engaku Taino and Yamada Mumon Roshi.

He authored on related subjects *Unhappiness, Sadness and 'Depression'* (2017), and *Psychotherapy, Mindfulness and Buddhist Meditation* (2019). Email: giraldi@units.it; tulliogiraldi@gmail.com. WEB page: http://www.tulliogiraldi.it/it_IT/. YouTube channel: https://www.youtube.com/@tulliogiraldi9290. Facebook: La Via di Mezzo.

1

Prologue

Zen Buddhism and the reality of suffering: a few words that seem to clearly define a theme, but which are at the same time deceptively simple, and actually open up a vast and complex world. The intention of this book is to offer a reasoned guide to that world: to the relationship between Zen Buddhism, the perspective and the means through which we access reality, and how we personally experience the sufferings, delusions and illusions which unavoidably accompany human life.

The literature on these subjects is enormous, and it is even more extensive if you consider adjacent or related areas, which cannot be avoided. Indeed, both within Zen and Buddhism and beyond, these topics have been explored and analysed by some of the greatest thinkers of the past.

The relevance of religion, philosophy and, based on recent developments, psychology is manifest. The subject is complicated, however, by the fact that Buddhist and Zen masters, monks and their experienced followers, believe it is only possible to truly understand Buddhism and Zen through sincere and deep practice, and that a scholarly or intellectual approach alone is inadequate.

Since the beginnings of Buddhism and Zen in northern India in the time of the historic Buddha, Siddhartha Gautama, their essence has been

T. Giraldi, *Zen Buddhism and the Reality of Suffering*,
https://doi.org/10.1007/978-3-031-69244-4_1

encrusted with layers of traditions and practices, as they spread through Ceylon, China, Japan and Southern Asia. Their recent diffusion through the West has added more interesting layers to the story, along with a peculiar contemporary phenomenon: the astonishing spread of mindfulness. Claiming to be rooted in Buddhist meditation, it promises simple and immediate means to staunch life's sufferings, particularly those associated with stress, and even claims to be effective for treating some mental disorders, mainly depression.

In the course of its 2500-year life, Buddhism has spread to a significant portion of the world, becoming the fourth largest religion, today followed by 7 per cent of the global population. While maintaining its original foundations, it has also integrated a constellation of different local traditions, developing into the Theravada Hinayana, Mahayana and Tibetan Vajrayana Schools, which have recently gained diffusion in the West too.

The historic Buddha himself is believed to have left no written teachings. In the centuries following his death, however, numerous large councils attempted to recollect and gather his sayings from oral traditions, and the result is a rich variety of texts. The Theravada collection, written in the Pali language, is compiled into three large groups called the Tipitaka, the 'three baskets'. It is possible to realise their sheer scale through the work of the Pali Text Society, which was established in 1881 in Bristol in the United Kingdom. Since its foundation, the Society has published 55 volumes of Theravada texts, translated into English.

Western interest in Buddhism developed substantially from the end of the nineteenth century, largely due to the spread of vast European empires into parts of the globe where Buddhism dominated. The British Empire, in particular, played a crucial role in increasing awareness of Asian religions including Buddhism. In the USA, too, with increasing numbers of migrants, Buddhist monks came, monasteries were founded, and before long, their practices began to flourish beyond Asian ethnic groups. These connections deepened and strengthened after the Second World War, when Westerners began to undertake the traditional training of Buddhist and Zen monks in Japan.

Western interest in Buddhism also grew substantially because of the influence of other, often unexpected fashions and cultural trends. In the

1960s, the hippie counterculture flourishing on the West Coast of the USA fostered a particular enthusiasm for Japanese Zen and its unique characteristics. As Westerners explored it, they discovered that different mental states were claimed to be achieved: old enlightened Zen masters, the *roshi*, had reached the transcendent state of *kensho* and *satori*, the *nirvana* of previous Indian traditions. Their disciples could reach these states, they discovered, through practice and by following the teachings of the masters.

Zen and Buddhism thus became ever more popular in the West. Psychologists and psychiatrists started to use Western scientific methods and technologies to explore the effect of Buddhist meditation on the brain and mind. Some even began to propose adding Buddhist meditation to the existing arsenal of psychological therapies.

Western interest was not limited to psychology and psychiatry, and other fields began to engage with the themes of this book, from religion and philosophy to neurosciences, to name but a few. There are, however, clear dangers in attempting to address such broad and profound subjects, including the risk of taking a potentially ingenuous, presumptuous and simplistic approach. It may, therefore, be appropriate to offer a few remarks about the author's individual experiences and competencies, and the role these will play in the following study.

Scientific and academic writings are generally presented in an impersonal and objective frame, where the author's individuality is set aside as being extraneous and potentially misleading and inimical to the objectivity of the study. This view is largely based on the notion that only rational impersonality can guarantee objectivity in science. At the same time, however, it is widely accepted that science is a complex construct, involving a constellation of factors, including subjective individual characteristics, personal accounts and emotional developments, as well as the prevalent intellectual and cultural values of the historical time. A direct, personal interview with an author may effectively enrich the traditional impersonality of a work, and the interest of this approach will be illustrated by some examples in a later chapter of this book. The author will therefore dwell briefly here on the experiences garnered through a lifetime in academia, scientific research, publishing, teaching, tutoring and training students and young researchers, along with the experiences of

Zen Buddhism relevant to the themes explored in this work. Following this brief parenthesis, the remainder of this book will be structured in the traditional, impersonal manner, with notes and references from the best available literature.

The main areas where the author was actively involved begin with pharmacology, with a degree obtained with a thesis on the newly discovered neurotransmitter serotonin. Pharmacology aims to treat human diseases as well as mental suffering and to elucidate the mechanisms of disease and of the effects of medicines. These purposes are pursued following rigorous procedures which guarantee a strict objectivity for the results obtained.

Alongside the academic career which followed, other experiences shaped my interest in the subject of this book.

The first one is a series of innovations in psychiatric care, which initiated in Gorizia, Italy, in the early 1960s by Franco Basaglia, who soon moved to nearby Trieste, where he was able to develop his approach on a larger scale. The basic principles for addressing the mental suffering of psychiatric patients were the respect and empowerment of patients, and a limited recourse to psychiatric treatments for which there was often only arguable scientific evidence of efficacy and safety. The aim of the interventions was focussed to restore patients to the best possible recovery, in terms of their own mental health and social integration. These principles proved feasible and effective, and despite the difficulties that might be expected because of the scale and radical nature of the reforms, they proved workable and were demonstrated to have very positive results. I participated actively also in terms of research to these experiences, and at the same time, I completed the training as a psychotherapist in transactional analysis, which I choose for its phenomenological and psychodynamic principles.

A second important and professionally relevant event was my experience with the ethics committees of the National Health Services (NHS) and of the University of Trieste, where I served as a member, later chairing them until my retirement. Ethics committee work was demanding and stimulating, since it involved examining research projects, discussing them with their proposers in various fields, mainly psychiatry. Only projects with a solid scientific base, with clear aims and endpoints, could justify the exposure of patients to the uncertainties of the trials for new treatments, and could be approved. A rich new world thus appeared, since most of the justifications provided often seemed plausible, yet were weak or inconsistent and inadequate to justify approval. The challenge of fitting the complexity of human conditions, diseases and treatments into a rigorous, objective and scientific frame became all too clear.

One final, crucial feature of my experience was my encounter with Zen, which was the beginning of a journey that would profoundly shape my whole understanding of existential and mental suffering and their treatment.

My first encounter with Zen occurred while I was a visiting researcher at the National Institutes of Health in Washington DC in the mid-1970s when I met a group affiliated with the Zen Study Society of New York, founded and directed by Eido Shimano Roshi, a Japanese Zen Master. Returning to Europe, the real breakthrough happened when I learned of the existence of a remote monastery in the hills near the town of Orvieto, in central Italy. Its name was *Zenshinji*, or locally, Scaramuccia. The founder and master was Engaku Taino, Luigi Mario, a Zen Rinzai master who trained in Japan at Shofukuji, and was authorised to teach Zen by Yamada Mumon Roshi, considered the last great Japanese Rinzai Zen master of our time.

I found my master and my place there, and in 1982, I was ordained as a lay monk with the name of Shiryo. In 1985, I spent a period in Japan, including a stay at Sogenji in Okayama, with the master of that monastery, Harada Shodo, also a disciple of Yamada Mumon Roshi. Over the years, I was formally recognised at Zenshinji as a Meditation and Dharma Master, and by the Italian Buddhist Union as a Minister of Buddhist Worship. During those years, I started a Zenshinji-affiliated Zen centre in Trieste, which was open in particular to undergraduate and postgraduate students in the medical and psychological professions, as well as subjects in the public health care system suffering from mental ailments.

This book is the third in a trilogy in the area of existential and mental suffering and their treatment, which includes the perspectives emerging from these experiences. The first, entitled *Unhappy, sad or 'depressed'*, considered the difficulty of distinguishing the mood variations arising from healthy responses to life events, from morbid, non-reactive endogenous states that require psychological and medical attention, including psychiatric medication.[1] The second, entitled *Mindfulness, psychotherapy and Buddhist meditation*, described the amazing beginnings of mindfulness in the USA, and its extraordinary growth and popularity also in Europe and numerous other countries.[2] It considers how the ancient Buddhist concept, *sati* in the Pali language, has been translated to *mindfulness* in English and spread to global fame and usage. It also analyses how it thus became substantially detached from the world of Buddhism and taken on a life of its own, coming to be incorporated into neurosciences and related cognitive and behavioural psychotherapies.

The basic idea of this book is to chart the evolution of the core Buddhist principles, and how they have transformed as they have been applied to the complex challenges of a modern globalised society whose values are based on individualism and mass consumerism. It seeks to explore how they have been applied to individual sufferings, the illusions and delusions of life, and their reality.

The first area to be explored, in Chap. 2, will be how Buddhism became one of the great religions alongside Judaism, Christianity and Islam. In the course of its 2500 years, Buddhism spread through large areas of Asia, where it diversified into several traditional schools and became integrated into numerous varied cultures. During this process, however, it maintained its core characteristics, which distinguish it as fundamentally different from the Abrahamic religions. Buddhism is non-theistic, and does not worship supernatural beings, sacred scriptures and revelations requiring formal adherence and faith from the believer. In a way, it has been defined as an existential and philosophical approach aiming to overcome the sufferings encountered in life. As such, Buddhism can be seen as transcending the characteristics of the other creeds. On the one hand, it satisfies the universal human needs of religiosity and spirituality, while on the other hand, it emphasises the natural individual experience, together with the inter-connection of all facets of reality and the cause-effect relationships binding them.

[1] Giraldi, T. (2017) *Unhappiness, sadness and 'depression': Antidepressants and the mental disorder epidemic*. Cham, Switzerland: Palgrave Macmillan.

[2] Giraldi, T. (2020) *Psychotherapy, mindfulness and Buddhist meditation*. Cham, Switzerland: Palgrave Macmillan.

Chapter 3, *Zen, Beyond Buddhism*, will examine in more depth the history of Zen Buddhism and its evolution as it spread from India to China around the sixth century AD. A new School, *Chan*, was established there by a monk named Bodhidharma, and it later spread as Zen to Japan and Southeast Asia. Then finally in the last century, it spread even further, to America and Europe. It is possible to understand the uniqueness of Zen immediately by looking at the Bodhidharma's definition: a special transmission outside the scriptures, not founded on words and letters, and which, by engaging directly with one's mind, allows one to see one's own true nature and thus attain enlightenment. It is evident what a radical shift this was from the essence not only of the doctrines of the other religions but even from the traditional schools of Buddhism themselves. This new, direct approach to the deeper aspects of human nature, enabling individual liberation from the constraints of life experiences, is unique, revolutionary, and shows how Zen is a step beyond the religious forms of the other Buddhist traditions.

Over time, Zen moved beyond Asia, and this is the subject of Chap. 4, *Zen Moves West*. Zen gained a remarkable place in Western culture when it became accessible to scholars and interested individuals at the end of the nineteenth century in the United States and the United Kingdom. Its remarkable characteristics immediately caught the attention of Western minds, showing as it did, a direct way of attaining enlightenment (awakening, *nirvana*, called *kensho* and *satori* in the Zen tradition), which ultimately means liberation from the constraints of the individual, unenlightened mind, and freedom from the existential sufferings of life. Progress along the Way was guided by Zen masters, the *roshi*, which were the living testimony of the enlightenment achieved through a lineage of transmission which went back to Shakyamuni Buddha. This enabled Zen to achieve wide popularity on the West Coast of the USA in the 1960s, contributing to the revolutionary and innovative culture developing there, then later spreading to other countries.

Among the first Western intellectuals to engage with Buddhism, it is not surprising to find psychologists and psychoanalysts, attracted by its promise to overcome life's sufferings. This is the subject of Chap. 5, *Psychology Discovers Zen*. These pioneering psychoanalysts came from a tradition that is strongly grounded in a humanistic perspective, where individual mental difficulties are psychodynamically related to subjects' life experiences. Soon, however, some psychologists and psychiatrists began to explore using Buddhist and Zen meditation for psychotherapeutic interventions, not only in the West but also in Japan. Researchers coming from a psychodynamically oriented, humanistic and person-centred perspective could begin to explore the human mind from the original and profound Buddhist perspective, which inspired their psychotherapeutic work.

Chapter 6, *The Mind and the Natural World: Buddhism, Science and the Reality of Reality*, deals with the question of the reality of the internal and external human worlds—and how this has been explored by the most brilliant thinkers and experimental scientists. Inevitably, the human mind begins to understand the inner and external worlds, when the data provided by the senses are processed by the brain, becoming partly available to the consciousness: the awareness of the natural world can only come through the filter of each person's individual experience. Even more difficult: when examining the inner world, the object of investigation is the same as the instrument by which the analysis is performed. The examination of mental activity is limited both by emotional modulation and by the existence of vast areas of the subconscious where it is stored that are simply inaccessible. In any given moment, the brain can only provide its conscious function with a limited selection from its wider inner processes. As such, reality can be seen as a product of selected parts of individual minds, a subjective product basically indistinguishable from a dream, a nightmare or a psychedelic experience produced by hallucinogenic drugs.

Modern sciences were developed in the seventeenth and eighteenth centuries in Europe, during the Age of Enlightenment, with dramatic intellectual progress and ensuing irreversible social consequences; this is the subject of Chap. 7, *Science and the Natural World: The Puzzle of Complex Non-Linear and Chaotic Phenomena*. The Enlightenment era was centred on a set of principles based on human reason and on physical evidence, which allowed us to abandon many of the superstitions prevailing until then and which laid the foundations for a modern understanding of natural phenomena through the new methods of experimental science. There has been irresistible progress in basic and applied science since then, which has profoundly and irreversibly reshaped the human relationship with the natural world.

The extraordinary progress made possible by the scientific revolution was destined, however, to reach some limits. For instance, when the experimental scientific method was used in psychology to study human behaviour and the mechanisms of the mind, it produced outstanding results, culminating in the recent flourishing of cognitive studies and neuroscience. Difficulties arise, however, when attempting to apply this same approach not to 'simple' phenomena governed by a single, linear cause-effect relationship but to 'complex' systems, attempting to treat them as simple phenomena, as commonly occurs in biology and psychology. Where a large number of factors are mutually interacting, the reaction of the system to modifying influences cannot be successfully described or predicted, since complex systems are subject to mathematically non-linear 'chaotic' interactions. These aspects are often overlooked when neurosciences and cognitive sciences attempt to describe aspects of human nature such as the suffering and mental ailments that arise in the course of most human lives. In molecular biology and brain imaging, there are often 'statistically significant' results, but their magnitude and relevance for the entire phenomenon considered remain elusive, particularly their practical and clinical relevance. There are certain areas where this is particularly significant, as shown in Chap. 8, *Mindfulness East and West: Cognitive Therapies and Biological Psychiatry*. After the Second World War, the developments in psychopharmacology led to the growth of biological psychiatry, which was destined to merge with the new developments in cognitive studies and neuroscience. Evidence-based somatic medicine became extremely important for understanding diseases and their treatments. The so-called biological psychiatry which developed after the Second World War had a similar focus, but the limitations of this field soon became clear. The nature of mental disorders was highly debated, and particularly their diagnosis, which did not benefit from the technological progress made in other fields of modern medicine. When interventions were made, the difficulty of identifying and diagnosing really morbid conditions became obvious. And, when drug therapy or psychotherapies were applied, evaluations of effectiveness were beset by the same difficulties. Biological psychiatry, neurosciences and cognitive therapies therefore met the criticism of having lost contact with the realities of the complex human condition and of employing inappropriately simple models of description and intervention that were considered reductionist and mechanistic.

An unexpected development at the end of the 1970s in the USA was Jon Kabat-Zinn proposal for mindfulness, Buddhist meditation without Buddhism. Mindfulness was destined to spread and gain a popularity that continues in the USA and Europe, largely beyond the traditional practice of Buddhism. The basic idea is simple: since life brings sufferings, and the aim of Buddhism is to extinguish life's suffering, meditation (deprived of any connection with Buddhism) can help people suffering from mental ailments. The theoretical basis of this, however, is tenuous since it implies that the aim of the demanding and carefully articulated totality of Buddhism can be pursued by extracting a small part of its practice and isolating it from its origins. Mindfulness interventions have been widely accepted in evidence-based medicine thanks to the efforts of Kabat-Zinn and his followers, who have striven to prove its effectiveness for controlling the negative consequences of stress, as well as a variety of mental conditions, especially depression. Mindfulness has also been integrated into recently developed varieties of cognitive behavioural therapies, where meditation has become marginal, and the overall approach has lost its humanistic and psychodynamic value.

Zen Meditation in an Open Public Mental Health Institution, Chap. 9, will explain what happened in an open public mental health institution in Trieste that has been offering zazen, Zen meditation according to the Rinzai tradition. This happened in a psychiatric institution originally called *Phrenocomion*, a sort of independent village beautifully built on a large green area at the border of the city by the Austrian empress Maria Theresia at the end of the eighteenth century. This is the place where, in the 1970s, Franco Basaglia, taking the position of director, developed and applied his innovative ideas for a new psychiatry. It now hosts the Department of Mental Health of the National Health Service together with Trieste University's Department of Psychology. As an ideal example of a place where people suffering from mental illnesses meet the psychologists and psychiatrists involved in their care, it is the perfect place to apply Buddhist principles and meditation as a mental health intervention.

Since 2014, it has been offering zazen, periods of quiet sitting meditation with moments of group sharing, to both patients and members of staff. The outcomes are extremely varied, and in several instances, the subjects abandoned the meditation group from the beginning. Other subjects, however, became deeply involved, with significant improvements in adaptation to distressing life events, which impressed the staff members involved. Common diagnostic criteria and psychometric scales were used but proved of little use considering the limited number of cases and the differences between people's individual experiences. For these reasons, the interventions have been mainly described as a narrative, which seemed the best way to convey the richness and variety of the individuals' existential and meditative experiences.

The *Epilogue*, Chap. 10, will consider how the effects of meditation on the brain have been examined using the powerful tools of modern science. Nevertheless, it remains challenging to imagine interventions that effectively bring together the world of Buddhism and that of the cognitive sciences and psychiatry, particularly the possibility of integrating the wisdom, morality and progression towards enlightenment that Buddhism provides beyond the limitations of the individual self. Zen offers the most direct approach, detached from creeds and beliefs, including those of the traditional scriptures of the various Buddhist Schools. It is fascinating to imagine the extraordinary achievements possible if scientific investigation could be merged with Buddhism and Zen in such a way as to preserve and integrate the humanistic, interpersonal and psychodynamic values involved.

Zen, with its unique and peculiar nature and its paradoxes, is still alive thanks to the efforts of enlightened, charismatic reformers. More recently, work has been done to render Buddhist meditation and Zen more accessible to modern times and society. Science provides extraordinary methodological tools, to better understand the *insight* sought by psychotherapies, and the *enlightenment* of Buddhism, as a natural state of the brain outside the rhetoric of scientific, spiritual and mystic approaches. Buddhism may contribute significantly to the de-medicalisation and de-psychologicisation of the non-morbid sufferings that arise from distressing life events, placing emphasis on an active personal role instead of passive adherence to diagnoses and prescriptions. Buddhism and science together might provide a new perspective about the natural states of consciousness: and Zen may have a special role to play because of its unique characteristics, the possibility of acquiring mindfulness through the mindlessness of *zazen*, Zen meditation. Modern society, and many of the technological developments arising from basic and applied science, present demanding challenges for consciousness, which may render the universal message of Buddhism more relevant than ever today.

This book will consider these subjects carefully and will guide the reader on a journey through the necessarily wide range of areas involved. In the course of this, great attention will be exerted to avoid slipping into a sort of pre-digested theoretical or practical guide and instead to aim to discuss these areas from the point of view of a detached, external neutral observer.

2

Buddhism, a Religion Beyond Religions

The history of humankind reveals the need for religions, and their dramatic, constant, pervasive and unavoidable role, from the appearance of *Homo sapiens* as a new species until the most recent developments in human society. Religions have accompanied and, in many cases, driven the development of human culture. For example, they have inspired some of the most astonishing human achievements yet have also been associated with, and even inspired, the worst episodes of organised intolerance, violence and war.

All human thoughts, behaviours and actions have their origins in the brain and its complex structure and functions. The human species is characterised by the massive development of the brain's cortex: the higher functions of the human mind, with their sophisticated elaborations such as abstract thought and symbolism, are believed to be localised to specific areas of the neocortex, operating in combination with those of the inner structures which are mainly responsible for most of the more basic and vegetative functions (Ackerman, 1992; Ernandes & Giammanco, 1998).

The brain is believed to be one of the most complex machines in the universe, because of the amazing number of its microscopic individual cells, the neurons, of which there are approximately 86 billion. This

T. Giraldi, *Zen Buddhism and the Reality of Suffering*,
https://doi.org/10.1007/978-3-031-69244-4_2

number is so great that it is reported to be approximately the same order of magnitude as all the stars in the Milky Way (Bradley, 2013). The number of connections between the brain neurons, the synapses, is estimated to be even greater: a mind-boggling 1000 trillion (Zhang, 2019).

This amazingly complex structure has provided the brain with similarly complex functions. In biological terms, the most basic are those of preserving the living state, and of guaranteeing the continuity of the life of the species through reproduction. The real jewel in the crown of the human species is the mind, which makes possible the most sophisticated human attributes. It allows the elaboration of the perceptions provided by the senses, and at a higher level, it is the instrument for the higher processes of thought: abstract conceptions and reasoning occur there, including those related to the religious domain such as spirituality and mysticism.

The regulation of the physiological functioning of the body, along with every thought and behaviour, is the result of mental processes occurring in the brain, which was shaped by the forces of the evolution of the species. Incidentally, the earliest writings of Charles Darwin, the founder of evolutionary theories, are not limited to the somatic traits of living beings and included the consideration of how psychological and religious phenomena might have been influenced by evolutionary processes (Mandelbaum, 1958; Person et al., 2016).

The timescale of the evolutionary events which moulded humans is very long and has to be measured in million years (MY); 55 MY for the first primitive primates, 5–6 MY for the first gorillas, chimpanzees and diverging human lineages, 2.5 MY for the emergence of *Homo habilis*. Our own species, *Homo sapiens* appeared 195,000 years ago (YA) and was endowed with an average brain volume of 1350 cm^3, comparable to the present one; 150,000 YA speech emerged, and archaeological evidence indicates that people developed complex speech and symbolism 100,000 YA (Pickrell, 2016). Forms of religiosity are ubiquitous in all known human populations and appear to be deeply and strongly embedded in the same human nature in a way which has been proposed to be part of the whole human constitution (Hamer, 2005).

The development of human culture has occurred in a very short time, measurable in tens of thousands of years, and from its beginnings, it evolved and spread to large parts of the planet with an astonishing speed which continues even today. The short space of time in which cultural evolution occurred means it cannot be ascribed to the same processes that drove the biological evolution of the species, which occurred over a much longer period. Biological mechanisms of a substantially stable nature appear to constitute the basis of cultural evolution, working in combination with the dynamic processes of cultural evolution; religions might have been involved in these processes.

Each of the great religions has offered extraordinary opportunities for spiritual and mystic individual experiences and offered to religiously inspired persons the opportunity to individually and collectively produce beautiful pieces of religious art, from tiny objects to colossal cathedrals. The religious values have at the same time led to the oppression of religious minorities within certain communities, and religious wars that have at various periods plagued large parts of the planet. Through proselytising, religions both spread themselves and also served to maintain temporal power, all based on their particular doctrines. Examining the vast and complex issues associated with faiths, intractable dichotomies between good and bad, right and wrong, are ubiquitous. And the beliefs and creeds involved are subject to temporal transformations, occurring in the context of dynamic changes to the complex phenomena of culture and society.

Archaeological examination reveals that religions have occurred in human history since the earliest preserved prehistoric human communities. An unceasing line of evolution from these initial stages continues, without interruptions, to the present, marked by the birth and death of cultures and religions, expanding and splitting in a never-ending process of schisms and conversions.

There are, however, some particularly revealing steps in the appearance and development of religions. Archaeologists have found burials among early Homo sapiens and Neanderthals dating from as far back as the middle palaeolithic or 100,000 YA, which are considered a primitive form of religious behaviour. And in terms of burials, by the ancient era, they come to take on the enormous proportions of the Egyptian pyramids. Most of the religions of the ancient civilisations were animistic and polytheistic, worshipping their own myths, idols, gods and goddesses, as happened at the beginnings of Roman and Greek ancient cultures. Some of the primitive religions went as far as introducing into their rituals, in addition to the worship of their symbols, even human sacrifices made in order to seek mercy and relief from calamities ascribed to their enraged deities (Smith, 2007).

The development of the Abrahamic, monotheistic religious movements Judaism, Christianity and Islam was destined to have a great and lasting impact, becoming the three biggest religious movements by population in the world. These three faiths shared the worship of a single deity, strictly maintaining at the same time their individual characters. Differentiations and schisms occurred within single faiths over a span of centuries, and also when they spread to different places and cultures, with Christianity a prominent example of this.

In Asia, religious movements followed completely different paths, which is perhaps unsurprising given the profound cultural differences between the West and India, China and Japan. For the latter two countries, their specific religious movements were also largely preserved by their relatively limited contact with Western cultures in ancient times by the strict limits imposed on material and intellectual exchanges with foreign cultures.

India was the cradle of Hinduism in the period beginning after approximately 1700 BC. The roots of these principles can be found in the oldest scriptures of the *Vedic* period starting somewhere between 1900 and 1400 BC. These early scriptures were later followed by *Veda* and *Vedanta*, and together with the *Upanishads* and the *Bhagavad Gita*, are considered the quintessence of Eastern thought and mysticism. It is from this deeply spiritual culture that other religions such as Buddhism later blossomed (Staal, 2017; Torwesten et al., 1991).

In India, Hinduism is characterised by a profound and universal spirituality, which is enriched by a number of gods and goddesses materially represented in statues and shrines that come in a rich variety of forms and colours. Chinese culture offered a completely different perspective, which was deeply rooted in the teachings of the Chinese philosopher Confucius (551–479 BC). It is a complex system of thought and behaviour which has been described as a tradition, a philosophy, a humanistic or rationalistic religion, a way of governing, or even just a way of life (Yao, 2010).

Taoism is another philosophy or religion that arose in China, and which emphasises living in harmony with the Tao, the source of everything and the ultimate principle underlying reality. The purpose of its practice is to become one with the unplanned rhythms of everything, called The Way or Tao, which is characterised by action without intention, with naturalness and simplicity. Taoism had a deep influence on various aspects of Chinese culture, such as alchemy, astrology, martial arts, traditional medicine, *feng shui* and *qigong*; it strongly influenced the development of Buddhism in China, and the school of *Chan* (Zen) Buddhism in particular (Wong, 2011; Weber et al., 1964).

Japanese culture, in spite of its geographical proximity to China, has profoundly different characteristics. One of the most quintessential Japanese faiths is Shintoism, an indigenous creed characterised by the absence of a central structure, and by a wide diversity of practices. Shinto is a polytheistic, animistic religion with supernatural entities called the kami believed to be present in all things and constituting a fundamental link between all natural entities. Shinto puts little emphasis on specific moral precepts and afterlife beliefs. It has no single creator or specific doctrine and exists in a range of local and regional forms. It has a large presence in Japan, with 100,000 public shrines, and it is numerically the second-largest religious movement after Buddhism. A further peculiarity is that Shinto beliefs and practices are not mutually exclusive of those from other religions, and a large part of the population of Japan shares both Shinto and Buddhist practices and activities, and festivals (Breen & Teeuwen, 2010; Teeuwen et al., 2003).

Buddhism has travelled far and wide in its long life and is considered the fourth religion in terms of number of devotees, following Christianity, Islam and Judaism (Johnson & Crossing, 2021). It is characterised by unique features, which are maintained throughout the various forms it has taken since its beginnings in Northern India: for these reasons, it deserves a place of its own among the other religions, which will be considered in more detail.

There is an extremely large scholarship on the history and universality of religion (Jones & Eliade, 2005; Doniger, 2006). The available evidence presents each religion as a collection of texts and traditions, which depends on the presence of one or more supernatural deities, their sacred relation to their religion, as well as a range of sacred scriptures and the revealed truth which they give to each creed.

There is a wide range of views, including from the best thinkers, about the value and meaning of religions and of atheism. There is a long way to go before such questions can be resolved, and it is arguable whether the human mind and its faculties are an adequate tool to resolve apparent dichotomies such as faith and reason, nature and the supernatural, and questions about the origins and nature of religions, spiritualism and mysticism.

Some of these issues have been re-examined and re-imagined recently by brilliant thinkers and deserve consideration (Stausberg, 2009). An original and provocative view about religion is offered by the philosopher Daniel Dennet in his book *Breaking the Spell*, subtitled *Religion as a Natural Phenomenon*. Dennett attempts to put religion into a scientific context and considers that religion always offered comfort to people in their suffering and inspired magnificent and terrible actions. He does not contest religious beliefs and rather seeks to uncover the origins of their power and discusses why and how different faiths have influenced so many lives. Ranging through biology, history and psychology, he argues about the psychological and cultural soil in which religions originated and evolved, and if they are the product of blind evolutionary forces or of individual rational choice, formed from individual superstitions, via shamanism and the early wild strains of religion, to today's institutionalised systems. The attempt is not antireligious and is rather aiming at a critical process away from established orthodox views (Dennett, 2006).

A similarly brilliant analysis comes from Richard Dawkins' 2006 book, *The God Delusion* (Dawkins, 2016). Dawkins is an evolutionary biologist and author who acquired great notoriety with the publication of his book *The Selfish Gene* (Dawkins, 1976). He subsequently published a series of bestselling books on science and philosophy, also presenting on television the positions he later adopted on the belief in God and its consequences, expressing them in a challenging and well-argued way. Dawkins is particularly concerned with the religious fundamentalism arising in the Middle East and in parts of America, and the dramatic consequences. The titles of his chapters give an idea of the topics considered from both historical and logical perspectives, for example, *The God Hypothesis and the Arguments for God's Existence, Why There Is Almost Certainly No God* and *The Roots of Religions, the Scriptures* (Dawkins, 2016).

Moreover, Dawkins introduced the concept of *meme*, small units of belief or behaviour, often endowed with symbolic value, which are transmitted from one mind to another during social interactions with mechanisms similar to those involved in the genetic evolution of biological traits (Dawkins, 2016). The role of *memes* has been studied by others, including Susan Blackmore, an eclectic psychologist who analysed the subject in her book *The Meme Machine* (Blackmore, 2000), in addition to her other studies on subjects such as consciousness and Zen (Blackmore, 2011). Considering the role that memes may have played in the process of cultural evolution, it is tempting to wonder what contribution they may have provided to the establishments of the religious creeds.

The themes considered offer a serious blow to many of the beliefs in the supernatural origins and sacred foundations of religious faith and lead towards a natural dimension which agrees with the thought of widely esteemed brilliant contemporary intellectuals such as Dennet and Dawkins.

The possibility that religious attitudes are simply a natural product of the human mind is clearly and strongly argued. The ideas of God and religion, in this argument, would be the product of a basic mechanism hardwired into the structure of the brain, developing in different ways depending on the social milieu and environment. They can and have been analysed with the tools of evolutionary biology, psychology and sociology.

One strong piece of evidence for this is the existence of the *cargo cults*, belief systems which have been observed in population groups indigenous to some areas of the Pacific Ocean, in which adherents perform rituals which they believe will cause a more technologically advanced society to deliver goods. This, it has been proposed, shows experimental evidence of the birth of a new religion right before the eyes of the observer. It has been taken seriously by several scientists, and Dawkins illustrates it in his book *The God Delusion*. Richard Feynman, the renowned Nobel laureate physicist, was so struck by the phenomenon of the *cargo cults* that he used the term in his lectures to refer to the many superstitious and unscientific beliefs which affect society in a negative and in many instances harmful way.

The *cargo cults* developed immediately after the Second World War and involved a large number of Melanesian islanders. The name derives from the observation of the activities of American armed forces, which arrived for the first time in remote places which had no previous contact with the Western civilisation. These foreigners built airplane runways and control towers; immediately after, numerous airplanes began to land, astonishing the locals with the delivery of a massive amount and variety of goods. After the end of the war, leaders immediately appeared, who established the belief that a range of ritualistic acts, such as excavating a strip intended as an airplane runway, or erecting a bamboo structure to simulate a control tower, would result in the appearance of material wealth on their islands, especially highly desirable Western goods (*cargo*) thanks to the arrival of airplanes. The cult had a vision of the future, particularly in times of crisis, as well as a charismatic figure who was the custodian and minister of its rituals.

This narrative is not unique. Another similar example is the John Frum cult from the island of Tanna, Vanuatu. This movement worshipped an American by the name of John Frum, who, it was claimed, had brought *cargo* to the island during World War II. He was seen as the spiritual entity who would provide *cargo* in the future. The characteristics of these cults are so peculiar that they have become key talking points in debates about religion and morality. Dawkins argues that this is evidence that religion is evolutionarily imprinted in our minds and that, in this context, the *cargo cults* might be regarded as the origins of a religion unfolding before our eyes (Attenborough, 2017; Dawkins, 2016).

Religious attitudes and behaviours largely appear to share a system of faith and beliefs, which promise either during this life or in an afterlife after death, relief and consolation for the afflictions encountered in everyday life, as well as punishment for prohibited actions. This brings in two themes which are central to this book: reality and existential suffering. Life continuously offers challenges, which are sometimes experienced as difficulty in adaptation to distressing life events, which cause individual subjective suffering. The challenge that arises is how real are the phenomena we are involved in and how real is the self of each individual living in their limited experience, the whole reality of the external and internal world.

In an extreme synthesis, the human species may be seen as the product of the evolution of primates, and human beings can be considered in a naturalistic and zoological perspective as *naked apes* as has been proposed in a popular and provocative way by Desmond Morris (Morris, 1994). In this analysis, modern human behaviour would merely be a development from the culture of hunter-gatherers living in small groups and mainly engaged in survival (Wade, 2007), leading to today when that behaviour appears in large organised societal groups, where intellectual values have gained a more significant role. Human behaviour, the external manifestation of the intellectual activity of the cerebral and mental world, can thus be examined in terms of its evolutionary meaning and purpose.

There is no doubt that the evolution of the brain to its present size and capacities is the most significant feature of the human species. It is the brain which permitted the extraordinary achievements of humanity and enabled it to shape the planet and its environments to an enormous extent. It is the same brain endowed with its extraordinary faculties which governs all of humanity's most remarkable activities, from the most moving acts of altruism and creativity to dreadful acts of violence and aggression. The religious spirit falls into this frame, and some of its most obvious markers are the relationship with the supernatural and divinity, worship of creeds through cults, symbols, scriptures and earthly prophets and ministers. These religious activities all point towards hope in the future and fear of and avoidance of suffering from life events. Another significant part of many cults is the practice of prayers to seek protection, as well as the absolution of sins to attempt to attain a peaceful life after death.

The fact that life necessarily brings us face-to-face with existential suffering is quite evident in unavoidable circumstances such as old age, disease and death. And it is remarkable to consider that the core messages of Buddhism are proposing a direct approach to existential suffering, facing the reality of the internal and external worlds, and finding a new way to adapt to them. In this way, they are completely different to the principles that characterise other religions.

The birth of Buddhism was an unexpected and unpredictable event amid the ubiquity and pervasiveness of religions. The history of Buddhism is long and complex, and to approach and represent its core meaning, a concise summary of some of its most unique aspects will be presented (Snelling, 1998; Trainor, 2004).

The tradition is that in the late spring of the year 531 BC, Prince Siddhartha Gautama Shakyamuni, in the Indian region of Bihar, achieved enlightenment, for which he has since been called the Buddha, the awakened. He immediately posed the question of whether and how to spread the truths he had understood, since they seemed to him so complex and innovative that they could be misunderstood. At first, he thought of turning to his former masters, but learning that they were dead, he decided to go in search of the five companions with whom he had shared six years of asceticism in the forest. After a long journey, he finally found them near Benares and received a cold welcome since they reminded him that he had renounced practising asceticism in its extreme forms, such as the maceration of the body. The Buddha then reminded them that the wisest and most useful attitude to keep in the search for truth is to proceed along a middle way, far from both exaltation and mortification of the pleasures of the body.

This can be considered a first general characteristic of his teaching: the search for truth must be pursued neither by pandering to the cult of pleasures nor by devising self-punitive practices. These two practices should not be avoided because they constitute a fault or because they derive from an original sin but because they represent harmful ways of distracting the attention from the search for truth. There is another immediately original aspect of the Buddha's teachings compared to those of other religions: he does not speak as God, nor as the Son of God, nor in the name of God, as his prophet. His words come from an entirely human experience, arisen from reflection on the problem of suffering. This problem is precisely spelled out in the famous *Sermon of Benares*, which constitutes the original nucleus of his teaching: the Four Noble Truths. They define the presence of suffering, its origin and the possibility to extinguish it through the eight precepts of the Eightfold Path or the Middle Way.

The historic Buddha, for 45 years until his death, taught everyone, men and women of all ages and of every social condition, without any religious and cultural discrimination, in the conviction that every person has in themselves the possibility of becoming a Buddha, an awakened. It is precisely this absence of discrimination that gives the Buddha's teachings the character of universality, and which allows us to see Buddhism as one of the great universal movements. There is another crucial difference between Buddhism and the Brahminic tradition that prevailed in India, where Buddha's teachings were imparted: it refuses to consider social differences as decisive for the practice and the attainment of enlightenment (Humphreys, 1951).

There is one more crucial, original feature of Buddha's teachings: a non-metaphysical attitude. This is conveyed clearly in the speech given to the Kalama. The *Kalama Sutta* is popular in the West due to its emphasis on free enquiry and rational thought and is frequently cited as the *Charter of Free Enquiry*. In this sermon, the Buddha addresses a group of people, the Kalamas of Kesamutta, who are not his followers and are not familiar with his teachings. They have sought the Buddha's advice because they have heard that he is a wise person. The Kalamas explain to him that they have been visited by many different spiritual teachers, each claiming to have the best teachings and also disparaging the views of other teachers. The Kalamas have been left confused and uncertain. They ask the Buddha whom they should trust. The Buddha advises:

> It is right that you have doubts and perplexities, because they are doubts related to controversial topics.
>
> Now, listen, O Kalama, do not be guided by rumours, traditions or hearsay; do not be guided by the authority of the religious texts, nor only by logic and inference; nor by consideration of appearances; nor by the pleasure of speculation; nor by verisimilitude; nor from the idea 'this is our teacher'.
>
> But, O Kalama, when you understand for yourself that certain things are not healthy, wrong and bad, then abandon them and when you understand for yourself that certain things are healthy and good, then accept them and follow them (Anguttara Nikāya, 1989).

This discourse is unique in its contents since it invites the listener not to be guided by traditions, religious texts, or teachers and not to indulge in speculations. It just encourages an individual experiential distinction between the wrong and bad and the healthy and good, in an anticipation of the moral perspective which is central to the Buddhist message. The Buddha advises against being guided by the authority of religious texts, even against the content of his teachings. They have to be regarded as an expression of a purely human experience, vast and profound, as the reflections of an exceptional individual who has travelled a particular way towards the truth and who wants to help others participate in the discoveries made along this path.

On these general premises, the Buddha's teaching and the whole of Buddhism could not build any system of dogmas and could, conversely, come into positive contact with religious cultures and with profoundly different traditions of thought. Buddha's teachings are quite unique in comparison with what is claimed by the other religious traditions. Since the teachings have to be considered non-sacred and since there is no sacred word to communicate and comment on, there is not even the legitimacy of a caste of priests professionally dedicated to these tasks.

The Buddhist teachers are individual monks who have set themselves on the path travelled by the Buddha with the aim of comprehending the truths that he experienced and formulated. Only the most gifted of monks could be considered masters, and even in this case, the master is only someone who has travelled before his students but also continues to travel, together with them, the road to the truth. The Buddhist master, rather than a repository of truth, should be a guide to the truth, who knows some dangerous steps and some fundamental practices to overcome them, but lets the disciple proceed with their own strength, without protecting them too much with some preconceived idea about the way and the goal, and without frightening them with terrifying stories about the difficulties of the way and the inaccessibility of the goal. In other words, in Buddhism, it is not a question of being under the tutelage of a *spiritual father* but rather a question of being in the company of *spiritual friends*.

The clear intention of the Buddha is to limit the claims of reason to explain questions in which there can be no empirical verification, such as the infinity of the universe, the immortality of the soul and the existence of the absolute. The reasons for preferring an experimental attitude over uncritical acceptance of some absolute truth are well illustrated in the *Parable of the Poisoned Arrow*. Here, the Buddha offers a comparison between a man who insists on seeking solutions to similar metaphysical questions and one who, wounded by an arrow, before being treated, wants to know from the doctor who struck him, to what family and caste he belongs, what his complexion, stature, place of birth and what kind of bow and arrow he used to hit him. It is evident that he would end up bleeding to death before having received satisfying answers to even one of these questions: thus, those who persist in wanting to find answers to metaphysical questions risk consuming their lives without being able to have that arrow, the metaphysical question, removed. At the end of his speech, the Buddha argues that whatever opinion one may have on the great metaphysical problems, there are still birth, old age, decay and death, suffering, pain, affliction and anguish, the cessation of which he offers a path to in this life (Cula-Malunkyovada Sutta, 1998). The Buddha's refusal to pronounce on the great metaphysical questions does not end with a nihilistic position but with the proposal to analyse the presence, nature and origin of pain, in order to be able to eradicate it or, at least, attenuate it during life. So, in general, this exhortation to the work of rational analysis rather than to the impulses of deistic enthusiasm can be well summarised with the words that indicate an invitation to *come to see*, not to *come to believe* (Pasqualotto, 2003).

In the preceding part of this chapter, reference has been made to the Buddha's discourses. It has to be noted that no written record of Buddha's teachings was made during his life by himself or his disciples, and after the death of the historical Buddha, they were only preserved through verbal transmission. Among the Buddhist monastic communities, however, there soon occurred doctrinal and disciplinary disputes, and they found it necessary to periodically convene to collect, print and revise them, and settle existing quarrels. These gatherings are often termed Buddhist councils; the first one is believed to have occurred after the third century BCE, and they continued periodically after, with the sixth occurring in Myanmar in 1954. In time, as Buddhism spread into Asia, particular traditions were established, and different canons evolved (Conze, 1959). The general term for the Buddhist scriptures is *Tipiṭaka* or *Tripiṭaka* (in Pali or Sanskrit, respectively), meaning *Triple Basket*, the traditional term for ancient collections of Buddhist scriptures (Lay, 2012). Some of the most important *Tripiṭaka* in the contemporary

Buddhist world are the *Pali Canon* maintained by the Theravada tradition in Southeast Asia, the *Chinese Buddhist Canon* maintained by the East Asian Buddhist tradition, and the *Tibetan Buddhist Canon* maintained by the Tibetan Buddhist tradition (Goonewardene, 1991).

The extreme breadth and variety of the forms that Buddhism has taken on is matched by the size of the scriptures known collectively as the Canons. What the Buddha really taught is a question which has been, and continues to be asked by devotees and scholars. Seeking a response is probably part of the progress along the *Middle Way*. One notable example is from Walpola Rahula, a Sri Lankan monk who in 1964 became the Professor of History and Religions at Northwestern University: he has written extensively about Buddhism in English, and one of his contributions is entitled *What the Buddha Taught* (Rahula, 2017). Another valuable contribution is that by Thich Nhat Hahn, a Vietnamese monk who was extremely active as a teacher, peace activist and author, with his book entitled *The Heart of the Buddha's Teachings* (Thich Nhat Hahn, 1999). A further interesting contribution is that provided by Akizuki Ryomin, a properly trained Japanese master in the Rinzai Zen tradition who also holds an academic position at the Hanazono University in Kyoto. In his book entitled *New Mahayana*, he addresses the issue of what the Buddha really taught and how his teachings have changed and are still changing while being integrated into contemporary Japanese culture (Akizuki et al., 1990).

There is, however, a common thread in the teachings of Buddhism, and a few key points about this will be considered here, leaving the following chapter to appraise how the Zen tradition blossomed from the mainstream of the other Asian Buddhist schools.

The starting point for an examination of the pillars of Buddhism is usually the *Setting the Wheel of Dhamma in Motion Sutra*, the discourse considered a record of the first sermon given by Gautama Buddha after his awakening in the deer park at Sarnath. Addressing his listeners, he explains the Four Noble Truths. Suffering derives from unavoidable life events such as birth, ageing, illness, death, union with what is displeasing, separation from what is pleasing, not to get what one wants. The easing and cessation of suffering thus requires the easing and cessation of the desire at the root of that suffering: the relinquishing of it, freedom from it, non-reliance on it; there is a way to the cessation of suffering, the *Middle Way*, and this is the *Noble Eightfold Path* (Soma, 1968).

The eight precepts are characterised by a marked moral dimension, all of them being preceded by the connotation *right*, that we have already encountered in the Buddha's discourse to the Kalama. They are enunciated in three sets. First, Wisdom: Right Thought (the realisation of the Four Noble Truths) and Right Understanding (the commitment to mental and ethical growth in moderation). Second, Moral Virtue: Right Speech (not hurtful, not exaggerated, in a truthful way), Right Actions (wholesome action, avoiding action that would do harm) and Right Livelihood (do not harm in any way oneself or others, directly or indirectly). Third, Meditation: Right Effort (effort to improve), Right Awareness (mental ability to clearly see things for what they are) and Right Concentration (deep meditation where the ego has disappeared and one reaches enlightenment). The Moral Virtue is intertwined with The Five Precepts, to which everybody should sincerely adhere, and which are combined with the resulting attitude that is attainable through their realisation, prescribing the abstention from killing living beings (kindness and compassion), theft (generosity and renunciation), sexual misconduct (contentment and respect for faithfulness), speaking lies (being honest and dependable) and intoxication (awareness and responsibility).

The brief summary below includes additional fundamental aspects:

The Three Jewels (Triple Gem, or Three Refuges) in which a Buddhist takes refuge at the beginning of the day or of a practice session, consisting of The Buddha (the fully enlightened one), The Dharma (the teachings expounded by the Buddha) and the Sangha (the community of Buddhists who practice the Way).

The Three Marks of existence, the characteristics of all existence and beings, namely the impermanence and emptiness, the non-self and selflessness and the sufferings of existence.

The Three Poisons, the Three Unwholesome Roots, the root of craving and suffering (with the animal indicated to represent them, and the attitude attainable through their realisation). Ignorance (delusion, confusion; pig) leading to wisdom; attachment (greed; bird) leading to generosity; aversion (hate; snake) leading to loving-kindness.

This outline obviously makes reference just to the denomination and does not consider the profound meaning of each of the issues indicated. It offers at the same time the opportunity to focus on some unique, important elements.

Even this superficial examination reveals the Middle Way's essential moral focuses and the important role of meditation in proceeding along the Way.

The importance of meditation, and the depth of Buddhist understanding of the mind and its obstacles, is clearly shown in the teachings of the *Satipatthana Sutta, The Great Discourse on the Establishing of Awareness*. This Sutta is at the core of traditional schools, such as the Theravada, and incidentally is a reference point for the recent Western mindfulness movement. It offers a clear aim and means to practice meditation. Its teachings are largely consistent with those of the other Buddhist schools, whose meditative practices differ mainly in terms of the contemplations to follow during meditation, or even in some cases the aim of mental emptiness. There are also variations in the specific traditions of the schools.

The essence of meditation as depicted in the *Satipatthana Sutta* is to stay sitting with crossed legs and body in an upright posture, concentrated on breathing. One is also advised to focus on contemplating the body and the sensations arising from the body, the mind and its contents. The Sutta warns the meditator of the difficulties they may encounter, which are the five hindrances: sensory desire, ill-will, sloth and torpor, restlessness and worry, doubt. Together with these negative factors, it also illustrates the seven factors which bring one towards enlightenment: awareness, investigation of Dharma, energy, joy, tranquillity, concentration and equanimity (Soma, 1998).

The *Anapanasati Sutta* (*Anapanasmṛti Sutra* in Sanskrit) also provides instructions for meditation that are consistent with those of the *Satipatthana Sutta*. This Sutta is also called *The Breath Awareness Discourse*, the Buddha's instruction for using one's awareness of breathing as an initial focus for meditation. Both Suttas are a reference to the Buddhist world, commonly made also by the Western contemporary mindfulness movement (Hahn, 2008; Nanamoli, 2010).

The core of Buddhist practice has been largely preserved and kept alive, even over the long period since its beginnings more than two millennia ago, and while it was incorporated into new countries, communities and remarkably varied cultural traditions where it took root. This continuity largely came about because of the transmission of teachings from master to master through uninterrupted lineages dating back to the historic Buddha.

It has to be noted, however, that the way Western scholars and devotees understand Buddhism today diverges substantially from the realities of traditional practice. In its original Asian forms, even devoted laypeople closely involved with the community of a Buddhist temple do not usually practise meditation, and most Buddhists only come into contact with monasteries for liturgies, mainly related to deaths and funerals, or less frequently for other spiritual reasons (Bodiford, 2007).

The formal practices of traditional Buddhist schools are followed only by a small number of novices, who undergo the hardships of time-consuming and rigorous training processes, which include long periods of meditation. In Zen, for example, only those motivated enough to spend ten or fifteen years training in a monastery complete their full training to become a master. The majority of novice monks limit their experience to the minimum residence of one to three years, before leaving the monastery to take charge of the family temple (Sharf, 1995a, 1995b). Based on historical evidence, it seems that in the West, traditional Buddhist practices are misrepresented and misunderstood, with a selected portion of their practices being taken for the whole. At the same time, however, there has also been a widespread urge to return to zazen or vipassana meditation, in no small part because of its religious development in the West.

It is therefore understandable that efforts have been made to render the Buddhist path more accessible to lay followers, particularly given the growing interest of new Western devotees and the spread of Buddhism to their countries.

In Japanese Zen, the *F.A.S. Society* was founded by the philosopher and lay practitioner Himasatsu Shin Ichi in 1958 to promote a transcultural non-religious approach; Himasatsu followers have never been great in number and are mainly present in Japan. Another innovative path came from Yasutani Hakuun in 1954, when he proposed the *SamboKyodan*. This had a greater impact, particularly on the lay practice of Zen in the

West, with one of the key purposes being rapid progress towards the attainment of awakening. There were also similar movements with some success in South Asia. The Theravada tradition in Sri Lanka, Myanmar and Thailand was reformed by Mahasi Sayadaw, in an attempt to give lay persons practicing meditation a smaller path towards enlightenment. This also suited followers in both Eastern and Western countries who sought less exacting requirements (Sharf, 1995a, 1995b). The topic of modernism has been analysed by David L. McMahan in his book *The Making of Buddhist Modernism*, which examines key aspects of Buddhism such as its discourses and traditions, the romanticism of its art, and spontaneity and nature. Meditation and mindfulness are also considered, together with their place in ordinary life, and even postmodernism (McMahan, 2009).

The problem of the accessibility of Buddhist teachings and their realisation has thus been addressed with numerous attempts at innovation, which have also sought to render the practice of Buddhism more accessible to the general population of the modern world. There is also substantial scholarship on these attempts.

Stephen Batchelor, a Scottish Buddhist, has been engaged with qualified teachers in the practice of the Tibetan tradition in India and Switzerland and of Zen Buddhism in South Korea. He later established himself in Europe, becoming a noted proponent of agnostic or secular Buddhism. His experiences are portrayed in the book *Confession of a Buddhist Atheist*, where he also presents his understanding of what the Buddha really taught (Batchelor, 2011a). Some of his other contributions can be cited here, such as *The Faith to Doubt: Glimpses of Buddhist Uncertainty* (Batchelor, 2015), *Buddhism Without Beliefs* (Batchelor, 2008), *The Awakening of the West: The Encounter of Buddhism and Western Culture* (Batchelor, 2011a, 2011b) and *After Buddhism: Rethinking the Dharma for a Secular Age* (Batchelor, 2017).

There is also David Brazier's exhaustive review of the different aspects that characterise modern Buddhism, *The New Buddhism* (Brazier, 2002). Several qualified authors also provide their contributions in *Secularizing Buddhism. New Perspectives on a Dynamic Tradition*, edited by Richard K. Paine (Payne, 2021).

The attention paid to Buddhism in the West is remarkable, and it has been likely enhanced by the contemporary *mindfulness* movement. Interesting contributions have been made by lay personalities too, such as Robert Wright's *Why Buddhism is True,* which is largely in favour of Buddhism (Wright, 2017). Evan Thompson, on the other hand, argues from a philosophical perspective in *Why I Am Not a Buddhist* that the current popular representation of Buddhism as a rational and scientific approach is simply untrue (Thompson, 2022).

Human evolution, both biological and cultural, seems to show a clear and deep-rooted need for a religious dimension, which has generally taken the form of displays of faith and the belief in the supernatural and the presence of deities, with whom sacred scriptures and ministers of faith have served as intermediaries. From this perspective, Buddhism is a unique phenomenon in that it has emerged as an existential approach that still satisfies that basic need for a religious dimension. At the same time, Buddhism avoids any recourse to the supernatural or theism, instead using existential, philosophical and psychological principles to emphasise the individual experience. Nevertheless, strictly, based on the framework laid out above, Buddhism can be seen as a religion, with its traditions and schools, scriptures, monasteries and temples, monks and masters.

Buddhism flourished transcending and detaching itself from the other religious creeds, and a new tradition developed from the body of Buddhism: Zen. This would strive to provide a new, direct way to awakening and enlightenment, the guide necessary to proceed along the Middle Way and realise enlightenment, at the same time avoiding the constraints caused by attachments to the ecclesiastical and scholarly constructions of the existing Buddhist schools, and this will be the subjects of the next chapter.

References

Ackerman, S. (1992). *Discovering the brain*. National Academy Press.

Akizuki, R., Heisig, J. W., & Swanson, P. L. (1990). *New mahāyāna: Buddhism for a post-modern world*. Asian Humanities Press.

"Anguttara Nikāya". (1989). *Oxford: Pali Text Society* (pp. 171–172).
Attenborough, D. (2017). *Journeys to the past: Travels in New Guinea, Madagascar, and the Northern Territory of Australia*. The Lutterworth Press.
Batchelor, S. (2008). *Buddhism without beliefs: A contemporary guide to awakening*. Bloomsbury.
Batchelor, S. (2011a). *Confession of a Buddhist atheist*. Spiegel & Grau Trade Paperbacks.
Batchelor, S. (2011b). *The awakening of the West: The encounter of Buddhism and Western culture*. Echo Point Books.
Batchelor, S. (2015). *The faith to doubt: Glimpses of Buddhist uncertainty*. Counterpoint.
Batchelor, S. (2017). *After Buddhism: Rethinking the dharma for a secular age*. Yale University Press.
Blackmore, S. J. (2000). *The meme machine*. Oxford University Press.
Blackmore, S. (2011). *Zen and the art of consciousness*. Oneworld.
Bodiford, W. M. (2007). Dharma transmission in theory and practice. *Zen Ritual* (pp. 261–282). https://doi.org/10.1093/acprof:oso/9780195304671.003.0010
Bradley, V. (2013). Are there really as many neurons in the human brain as stars in the milky way? *Nature news*. Nature Publishing Group. Retrieved October 26, 2022, from https://www.nature.com/scitable/blog/brain-metrics/are_there_really_as_many/
Brazier, D. (2002). *The new Buddhism*. Constable Robinson.
Breen, J., & Teeuwen, M. (2010). *A new history of Shinto*. Wiley-Blackwell.
Conze, E. (1959). *Buddhist scriptures*. Penguin Books.
Dawkins, C. R. (1976). *The selfish gene*. Oxford University Press.
Dawkins, R. (2016). *The God delusion*. Black Swan.
Dennett, D. C. (2006). *Breaking the spell*. Allen Lane.
Doniger, W. (2006). *Britannica Encyclopedia of world religions*. Encyclopaedia Britannica, Inc.
Ernandes, M., & Giammanco, S. (1998). Maclean's Triune Brain and the origin of the 'immense power being' idea. *Mankind Quarterly, 39*(2), 173–201. https://doi.org/10.46469/mq.1998.39.2.3
Goonewardene, A. D. (1991). *The Buddhist councils*. Buddhist Society.
Hahn, N. (1999). *The heart of the Buddha's teachings*. Rider.
Hahn, N. (2008). *Breathe, you are alive! The Sutra on the full awareness of breathing*. Parallax Press.

Hamer, D. (2005). *The God gene: How faith is hardwired into our genes.* Anchor Books.
Humphreys, C. (1951). *Buddhism.* Penguin Books.
Johnson, T. M., & Crossing, P. F. (2021). *The world by religion.* Brill. Brill. Retrieved October 27, 2022, from https://doi.org/10.1163/2589742X-12347111
Jones, L., & Eliade, M. (2005). *Encyclopedia of religion.* Macmillan Reference USA, Thomson Gale.
Lay, K. (2012). *Guide to tipitaka.* Buddhist Cultural Centre.
Mandelbaum, M. (1958). Darwin's religious views. *Journal of the History of Ideas, 19*(3), 363. https://doi.org/10.2307/2708041
McMahan, D. L. (2009). *The making of Buddhist modernism.* Oxford University Press.
Morris, D. (1994). *The Naked Ape Trilogy: The Naked Ape; the Human Zoo; intimate behaviour.* J. Cape.
Nanamoli. (2010). *Mindfulness of breathing—Urban dharma.* Retrieved from October 29, 2022, from https://www.urbandharma.org/pdf1/Mindfulness Breathing.pdf
Pasqualotto, G. (2003). *Il Buddhismo. I sentieri di una religione millenaria.* Bruno Mondadori.
Payne, R. K. (2021). *Secularizing Buddhism: New perspectives on a dynamic tradition.* Shambhala Publications, Inc.
Person, et al. (2016). The evolution of Darwin's religious faith—Article. *BioLogos.* Retrieved October 26, 2022, from https://biologos.org/articles/the-evolution-of-darwins-religious-faith
Pickrell, J. (2016). Timeline: Human evolution. *New Scientist.* Retrieved October 26, 2022, from https://www.newscientist.com/article/dn9989-timeline-uman-evolution/
Rahula, W. (2017). *What the Buddha taught.* Motilal Banarsidass.
Sharf, R. (1995a). Buddhist modernism and the rhetoric of meditative experience. *Numen, 42*(3), 228–283. https://doi.org/10.1163/1568527952598549
Sharf, R. H. (1995b). Sanbōkyōdan: Zen and the way of the new religions. *Japanese Journal of Religious Studies, 22*(3–4). https://doi.org/10.18874/jjrs.22.3-4.1995.417-458
Smith, L. S. (2007). *The illustrated timeline of religion: A crash course in words & pictures.* Sterling.
Snelling, J. (1998). *The Buddhist handbook: A complete guide to Buddhist schools, teaching, practice, and history.* Barnes & Noble Books.

Soma. (1968). *The Buddha's first discourse: Dhammacakkappavattana Sutta: With the Pali text*. Buddhist Publication Society.
Soma. (1998). *The way of mindfulness: The Satipatthana Sutta and its commentary*. Retrieved October 29, 2022, from https://www.accesstoinsight.org/lib/authors/soma/wayof.html
Staal, F. (2017). *Discovering the Vedas: Origins, mantras, rituals, insights*. Penguin.
Stausberg, M. (2009). *Contemporary theories of religion: A critical companion*. Routledge.
Teeuwen, M., Breen, J., & Satoshi, I. (2003). *Shinto, a short history*. RoutledgeCurzon.
Thanissaro Bhikkhu. (1998). *Cula-Malunkyovada Sutta: The shorter instructions to Malunkya*. Retrieved October 27, 2022, from https://www.accesstoinsight.org/tipitaka/mn/mn.063.than.html
Thompson, E. (2022). *Why I am not a Buddhist*. Yale University Press.
Torwesten, H., Phillips, J., & Rosset, L. (1991). *Vedanta: Heart of Hinduism*. Grove Press.
Trainor, K. (2004). *Buddhism: The illustrated guide*. Duncan Baird.
Wade, N. (2007). *Before the dawn: Recovering the lost history of our ancestors*. Penguin Books.
Weber, M., Gerth, H.-H., & Weber, M. (1964). *The religion of China Confucianism and Taoism*. Macmillan Co.
Wong, E. (2011). *Taoism: An essential guide*. Shambhala.
Wright, R. (2017). *Why Buddhism is true*. Simon & Schuster.
Yao, X. (2010). *An introduction to Confucianism*. Cambridge University Press.
Zhang, J. (2019). *Basic neural units of the brain: Neurons, synapses and action potential*. arXiv.org. Retrieved October 26, 2022, from https://arxiv.org/abs/1906.01703#:~:text=On%20average%2C%20the%20human%20brain,many%20as%201%2C000%20trillion%20synapses

3

Zen, Beyond Buddhism

Buddhism originated in the fifth century BC in Northern India, where the historic Buddha, Siddhartha Gautama, also called Shakyamuni, the awakened, imparted his teachings. In the following centuries, Buddhism spread far and wide across Asia, including modern-day Sri Lanka, Myanmar, Thailand, Laos and Indonesia through a route called the Southern transmission. It also reached to China, Vietnam, Korea, Japan and Tibet through the Northern transmission.

As it spread, Buddhism embraced profoundly different features from the communities where it took root, adapting to the spiritual needs of its new followers. Nevertheless, Buddhism retained its core features, creating a unique situation where the people's spiritual and religious needs were met, without appealing to deities and the supernatural.

The history of Buddhism extends across an extremely long time-span, in which it became established in hugely varied cultures. There is therefore extensive literature on this history, covering the full breadth of religious rites and ceremonies in all these traditions. There are also doctrinal and popularising contributions from Buddhist religious authorities, as well as lay devotees and academic scholars. This abundant literature offers many perspectives on the history of Buddhism, which vary based on the

T. Giraldi, *Zen Buddhism and the Reality of Suffering*,
https://doi.org/10.1007/978-3-031-69244-4_3

different aims, experiences and practices of the authors (Dumoulin, 1963; Snelling, 1999; O'Brien, 2019).

After its spread across Asia, there was one more remarkable development to come for the world of Buddhism: the arrival of Zen Buddhism. Characterised by singular features, Zen was to add substantially to the overall distinctiveness of Buddhism from other widespread religions.

Linguistically, the term *Zen* is an abbreviation *zenna*, which is a Japanese transliteration of the Chinese term *channa* which is, in turn, derived from the Sanskrit word *dhyana,* which means simply meditation. Therefore, when we speak of Zen Buddhism, we mean, literally, that form of Buddhism that emphasises meditation ahead of the theoretical discussions, the doctrines, the canonical texts and the ceremonial rites that characterise, to varying degrees, the other Buddhist Schools.

The linguistic progress from *dhyana* to Zen also faithfully traces, with some flecks of legend, the historical passage from early Buddhist Schools to Zen Buddhism. It seems, in fact, that around 520 AD, a great Indian Buddhist master, Bodhidharma, arrived in China, where he began to spread a particular form of Buddhism focused mainly on meditation, the *Chan*. This form of Buddhism was easily grafted onto the Chinese tradition of Taoism thanks to the work and teaching of the Chinese Master Hui Neng (638–713). The combination of Taoism and an Indian Buddhist tradition focused on meditation proved fruitful and led Chan Buddhism to spread widely, eventually reaching Japan. This was in particular because of the work of two masters. The first, Eisai Myoan (1141–1215), went to China to study with Master Huaichang, who, in 1191, gave him a certificate approving his right to teach, the *inka*. That same year, Eisai returned to Japan, where he founded Shofukuji, considered the first temple of Zen Buddhism. The School founded by Eisai was called *Rinzai*, a Japanese transliteration of *Lin-chi*, the name of a great master of Chan Buddhism, who died in the year 867. The second master, Dogen Eihei (1200–1253), after a long stay in China with Master Rujing (1163–1228), returned home and founded the Soto School.

Zen developed as a path to Buddhist awakening, stripped of most of the religious paraphernalia of the existing Buddhist traditions. At the same time, Zen also had a significant influence on the cultures in which it was practised, particularly in Japan. Several disparate Japanese traditions, including samurai swordsmanship, archery, *ikebana*, *aiku* and the tea ceremony, were profoundly influenced by Zen (Suzuki, 1970). And when, later, Buddhism moved West, it was once again Zen that received the most attention and fused with other cultural practices to meet the spiritual needs of occidental society.

This initially happened thanks to the translation of many Japanese texts that had previously been inaccessible to Westerners, by Daisetz Teidaro Suzuki, someone who himself had substantial first-hand experience of the practice of Rinzai Zen with various master teachers in Kyoto. Among his numerous books, *An introduction to Zen Buddhism,* with a foreword by Carl Gustav Jung, deserves particular attention (Suzuki, 1964). A number of other authors have made significant contributions to the substantial and growing Western interest in Zen, including Reginald Horace Blyth (Blyth, 1988), Alan Watts (Watts, 1962) and Philip Kapleau (Kapleau, 1967). Zen has also attracted the interest of writers and poets of the beat generation, including Jack Kerouac (Haynes, 2005), Allen Ginsberg (Miles, 1989) and Gary Snyder (Snyder, 2014). Influential psychologists such as Eric Fromm have also played their part (Suzuki et al., 1960).

The question we must now turn to is what Zen really is and how its practice is organised. This subject, however, offers challenges similar to those encountered when attempting to outline what the historic Buddha really taught, and the core teachings that were meant to be followed by Buddhist devotees. Bearing these considerations in mind, I will now address some of the key elements of Zen Buddhism, which are shared by the various Schools and traditions that developed from the origins of Zen.

Bodhidharma's description of Zen is brief but definitive:

> A special transmission outside the scriptures, not founded upon words and letters; by pointing directly to one's mind it lets one see into one's own true nature and thus attain Buddhahood (Dumoulin et al., 1990).

This definition suggests that Zen is characterised by anti-intellectualism, anti-dogmatism and attention to spontaneity and simplicity, and these are the core principles that will always set it apart. As expressed by Bodhidharma, these principles are clearly reminiscent of the discourse of

Shakyamuni Buddha to the Kalamas, in which he declares that one should deal with the sufferings of life by avoiding the use of scriptures, words and letters, and also of logic, inference, speculation and even to turn to a teacher.

Bodhidharma's definition of Zen clearly focuses on the fundamental aspects of the *Dharma transmission.* Zen has to be offered as a guide to other sentient beings to enable them to reach their own awakening themselves.

Buddhahood, in Bodhidharma's words, means reaching enlightenment, which in the Japanese tradition is called *kensho* and *satori*, the first experience of one's true nature obtained through Zen, and its deepening after prolonged practice giving a clearer vision of the inner and outer world.

Awakening, kensho and satori are central to the living experience and realisation of Zen teachings. This is clear from the Four Vows which Zen shares with most existing Buddhist traditions and which appear in various sutras. Also called the Bodhisattva Vows, they have a clear moral and altruistic dimension, implicitly excluding a selfish, solipsistic and narcissistic approach to enlightenment. Ritually chanted in Zen monasteries in the morning recitation, they are:

> However innumerable all beings are, I vow to enlighten them all;
> However inexhaustible my delusions are, I vow to extinguish them all;
> However immeasurable the Dharma Teachings are, I vow to master them all;
> However endless the Buddha's Way is, I vow to follow it. (Gyatso, 1991)

Zazen, sitting in quiet meditation, is the distinctive feature of Zen practice, and it follows the principles of meditation as set out in the Noble Eightfold Path of the Middle Way, requiring Right Effort, Right Awareness and Right Concentration.

Since the first days of Zen in Japan, two schools, the Soto and the Rinzai, followed slightly different approaches. The most well-known difference between them is the fact that the Soto School considers enlightenment the result of a gradual process of perfection based exclusively on silent, deep meditation. The Rinzai School on the other hand considers enlightenment a sudden event, which can occur when combining the practice of zazen sitting meditation with the *koan*, paradoxical questions, the solutions to which must be given privately to the master in regular individual meetings called *sanzen*.

There is extensive literature on the other differences between the schools. The Soto School, which has been dubbed 'the farmer's Zen', concentrates mainly on ritual prolonged immersion in sitting meditation, the Right Concentration, the *samadhi* of *shikantaza*, of the Middle Way which gradually leads to enlightenment. The main exchanges between the master and their disciples occur during *mondo*, formal question-and-answer sessions about meditation practice, which are held after zazen.

Rinzai Zen, also known as 'the samurai's Zen', places particular emphasis on the use of koans and stresses the importance of periods of activity both inside and outside the monastery, called *samu*. Novices, once accepted as monks, are asked to attend regular *sanzen* and try to answer their *koan* to show their grasp of Zen.

Before considering these core elements of Zen in more detail, it is worth recalling the emphasis that the very name places on meditation over all other aspects of Buddhism and that it is not something to be practiced solely in particular times or places; enlightenment can be achieved at any time, in any place and during any activity of daily life. To know Zen, one should practice it, not conceptualise it: one should experience it directly rather than talking or writing about it. On the other hand, it is also true that Zen has been transmitted to us not only through practice and imitation, but thanks to the writings and transcriptions of the masters' teachings. It is worth noting, for instance, that Dogen, the greatest proponent of pure meditative practice uncontaminated by spoken or written words, is also the author of *Shobogenzo*, a highly dense work of 95 chapters. It is also noteworthy that early on, Dogen also made extensive use of the koans and later abandoned them quite possibly in an attempt to clearly differentiate Soto from the Rinzai School (Pasqualotto, 2003; Heine, 2004).

This is one of the seeming contradictions of Zen that we must face in order to contend with the fact that you are at this point reading a written work about it, and we must also recognise that writing, like any other aspect of everyday life, can contribute to self-knowledge. There is a similar paradox in Buddha's discourse to the Kalamas, where Shakyamuni discourages addressing oneself to a teacher, at the same time as acting as a teacher himself and bringing in the unavoidable distinction between good and bad, and individual moral responsibility.

One of the most profound differences between the Soto and Rinzai schools is their emphasis on either gradual or sudden enlightenment. The Soto tradition, by using prolonged deep sitting meditation, as well as question-and-answer *mondo* sessions with a master, works towards gradual enlightenment. Rinzai practice is more varied and, by meditating on koans, strives towards opportunities for sudden awakening. Alongside sitting meditation on koans, it also involves engaging in meditation during daily activities such as work (*samu*), mondo sessions of questions and answers with the master, and lectures on select scriptures (*teisho* and *koza*), as well as exhortations (*junkei*). Followers of this school are thus under a constant, profound pressure, which has been dramatically depicted in a classic text by the great historical Zen masters.

It would be futile to attempt to debate the merits and demerits of the two schools. One may indeed have moments of profound realisation about one's true nature over the course of long and monotonous periods of meditation. Indeed, at the beginning of *Song of Zazen*, Hakuin Ekaku, an important seventeenth-century Rinzai master, declares:

> All beings from the first are Buddhas, having a kinship like water and ice; there can be no ice apart from water, no Buddhas apart from living beings.
>
> The merit of sitting even a single time cancels out the measureless evil karma, you will never enter the wrongful path, the Pure Land will never be far away! (Yamada & Waddel, 2021).

On the other hand, just sitting in meditation may not be sufficient to progress along the way to enlightenment, as Dogen noted in his thirteenth-century work *Shobogenzo*, in a chapter called *Admonitions for Zazen* (Dōgen, 1988). The exchanges between master and pupil have a characteristic Zen style:

> Nangaku picked up a broken piece of tile and began polishing it with a stone.
>
> When Kosei saw that he said, 'Master, what are you doing?'

Nangaku said, 'To polish it into a mirror'.
Kosei said, 'How can you make a mirror by polishing a tile?'
Nangaku said, 'How can you become a Buddha by doing Zazen?'

Rinzai training involves varied activities requiring the deepest possible concentration, and disciples meditate on koans. When a disciple satisfies their master with their answer to their first koan and attained *kensho,* a state beyond verbal consciousness, they receive their next koan to deal with.

The *Mumonkan*, a thirteenth-century text by Zen master Mumon Ekai, provides a taste of Rinzai Zen's approach to the relationship between writing and awakening. It is a collection of 48 cases to be used as koans, and Mumon added to each a verse and a comment: the title *Mumonkan* is translated as *The Gateless Gate*. In the preface, Shuan Chinken paradoxically invites not to use the Mumonkan. This advice is followed by that of Mumon, that Buddhism makes mind its foundation and no-gate its gate, and those who try to understand through other people's words, are scratching a shoe, whereas it is the foot that itches (Snelling, 1999).

This is a representative sample of Zen doctrine, a way of life embedded in monasteries and temples where traditions were preserved and passed down not through the written word but by direct monastic training down the generations.

In the centuries following the initial arrival of Buddhism and Zen in Japan, a large number of monasteries, temples and shrines were founded. It is estimated that approximately 77,000 temples were established, most often wooden buildings that are sometimes of extraordinary beauty and which have become national treasures (Wu, 2020).

Monasteries were places where masters, monks and novices lived and kept the Zen traditions alive. The Zen master who led each monastery would impart his teachings to his disciples, following Bodhidharma's principle of direct, heart-mind Dharma transmission from teacher to pupil. Enlightenment, the realisation of Buddhahood, was the focal point of the Zen experience; it was a prerequisite for the master, so they could transmit that realisation to their disciples. In the original Zen texts and traditions, therefore, there are many depictions of transmission from master to disciple to accomplish kensho and satori.

In Rinzai Zen, enlightenment was formally recognised by the *inka sonmei*, a sort of certification given by the master of the Dharma transmission, which allows the recipient to become a teacher, entering the specific lineage of their master and eventually becoming their successor.

This allows us to see Dharma transmission as the succession from the historic Buddha Shakyamuni, through all the masters, in sequence, up to the last living master of a monastery. This lineage is held in the highest reverence, and every morning in Zen monasteries, monks chant the series of names from the early patriarchs to the previous master of the monastery.

In fact, the idea of directly receiving the teachings of the certified master in charge of the monastery, an enlightened person who has already attained satori, is almost certainly one of the main attractions of Buddhist monasticism for new initiates. Inclination towards a monastic life, defined by adherence to Buddhist principles, may be an additional factor.

Daily life in Zen monasteries is strictly and ritually organised on the same daily schedule throughout the year—a programme that has been meticulously preserved throughout the history of Zen. Following Daisetz Teitaro Suzuki's description of these routines may be the most effective means of tracing the traditional training of a Zen monk, without having to resort to abstract conceptualisations.

D.T. Suzuki is a crucial author on this subject, whose works have been studied in detail elsewhere. Here, it will suffice to note that D.T. Suzuki provided the first translations of innumerable Japanese texts that had been previously inaccessible to Westerners. Moreover, his writings are those of a Japanese Buddhist who trained under the guidance of the renowned Zen masters of his time and decided not to restrict himself to monastic life but rather to make Zen Buddhism known to the West (Giraldi, 2020).

D.T. Suzuki provided a uniquely concise and incisive book, *An Introduction to Zen Buddhism*, with a foreword by C.G. Jung (Suzuki, 1964), which, together with his *The training of the Zen Buddhist Monk*, offers a unique vision of life in a Zen monastery (Suzuki, 1934).

This latter little book, first published in 1934, provides a sort of living testimony of how the Rinzai Zen monks were trained, in a text that instead of delving into abstract considerations, offers a wealth of anecdotes and Zen stories, and is enriched by 43 delightfully vivid illustrations that give a true flavour of the world Suzuki conveys. The chapters of the book are crammed with numerous Zen anecdotes and cover all aspects of the monks' lives: initiation and a life of humility, labour, service, prayer, gratitude and meditation. The series of descriptions begins with the pilgrimage to the monastery, followed by the steps of admission, asking for admittance and staying in the lodging room, which is initially formally refused. Then, after a formal waiting period, the applicant is initiated to the zendo and introduced to the Roshi. This is followed by scenes in the monks' daily life outside the monastery, ritually proceeding through the streets humbly collecting donations. It also traces their daily work of sweeping and gardening, followed by cooking and dining, nursing the sick, sewing and moxa-burning, shaving and washing.

The chapter on meditation includes many important details about the practice, which is strictly articulated and demanding, being scheduled throughout the full year. When the residing monks are not actually engaged in outdoor work, they are invariably found sitting in meditation in the zendo; they may briefly visit their family four times a year. Every month, there is a week, called *sesshin*, when the monks are exempt from work and practise zazen from early morning (3.30 a.m.) till evening (9.30 or 10 p.m.), except when they eat and when they attend the discourses on Zen textbooks. Four times a day, there is *sanzen*, where the monks see the master in his room to present the responses to their koan. If they do not yet have one, they go *dokusan*, individual and voluntary *sanzen*. Three times, while the sesshin is going on, no monk is allowed to stay away from seeing the master, and this may even be enforced, since seeing the master is central for Rinzai Zen.

The essential aim of the practice is awakening, the realisation of Buddhahood, following the altruistic practice of a Bodhisattva, through zazen and koans. It is worth examining this in more detail.

The Rinzai tradition explicitly refers to kensho as an awakening which must be formally demonstrated and satisfy the master during sanzen. Over the centuries in which the traditions and rituals of Zen have been formally practised, the koans have been grouped into a number of collections to be studied and passed, in succession, by disciples. With time, as one of the leading figures of Zen, Hakuin Ekaku (1686–1768) realised, in the eighteenth century, it became necessary to reassess the practice of the koans (Waddell, 1994).

Zen Dust: History of the koan and koan study in Rinzai (Linji), by Isshu Miura Roshi and Ruth Fuller Sasaki, is considered the most comprehensive resource on this subject available in Western languages. Both authors are unique individuals with impressive experience and qualifications. Isshu Miura was the abbot at Rinko-in, a temple in Shokokuji in Kyoto, where several Westerners have studied, among them R.H. Blyth, a British author and expert on Japanese culture, as well as the complex and multi-faceted Gary Snyder. Ruth Fuller Sasaki (1892–1967) was a pioneer who successfully contributed to the introduction of Zen to the United States where she was a strong supporter of Buddhism and helped to develop and establish in New York what would become the First Zen Institute of America. She was also actively involved in establishing a connection with Japan to facilitate and support the study of Rinzai Zen for foreigners. In 1949, she went to Kyoto where she stayed for most of the rest of her life; in 1958, she was recognised as the first Westerner, and the only woman, to be a priest and a master at Daitokuji temple, one of the main Rinzai institutions. She has been mainly engaged in the work of spreading Zen to the West and in translating numerous Zen texts into English (Stirling, 2006; Anderson & Schwartz, 2018).

Zen Dust is thus distinctive because of the profound expertise of its authors, Isshu Miura and Ruth F. Sasaki, and for the many detailed notes that accompany the text, along with drawings by Hakuin and genealogical charts of Zen lineages. The first two parts cover in great detail and accuracy the history of the study of the koans; the remaining larger part deals with the so-called *capping phrases*, which in traditional koan study had to be presented during sanzen to the master in order to fully complete the demonstration of a koan before receiving the next one (Miura & Sasaki, 2015; Hori, 2010).

The practice of koan study, together with that of capping phrases, is also extensively explored in the book *Zen Sand. The book of capping phrases for koan practice* by Victor Sogen Hori. The author, a PhD in philosophy from Stanford, was ordained a Zen monk, training in Rinzai Zen for 13 years at Daitokuji in Kyoto; in 1990, he returned to Canada where he joined the staff at the Faculty of Religious Studies at McGill University (Victor Sogen Hori, 2022).

There is also a collection of essays on koans by John Daido Loori, with a foreword by Thomas Yuho Kirchner, called *Sitting with koans: essential writing on Zen koan introspection*. The chapters are written by qualified contributors, with various different spiritual and academic experiences in Buddhism, covering a historical perspective, the Japanese study of koans, as well as modern koan commentaries (Loori, 2012).

There is also a practical introduction to Rinzai Zen training, meditation and koans, *Introduction to Zen training*, written by the deeply experienced master, Omori Sogen (Sogen, 2020).

There are several classic collections of koans that have been used for koan study, particularly since Hakuin's reforms. One of the most well-known is the *Mumonkan*, which has already been mentioned. It has been used since the thirteenth century for the training of monks and is well known for introducing the notion of *the gateless gate* to describe the barrier one has to pass through to reach kensho. A similarly well-known text is the *Hekiganroku*, *The Blu Cliff Records* (Sekida et al., 2005).

An important and perhaps less known contribution to koan study is that provided by the translation of the *Shumon Kattoshu*, the only major koan text to have been compiled in Japan rather than China, which contains 272 cases with extensive annotation, and which adds to the central koans of the contemporary Rinzai koan curriculum. The present translation arose from discussions between several Japanese Zen masters and the author Thomas Yuho Kirchner, an American-ordained Zen monk residing in Japan since 1969 (Kirchner, 2019).

The most important and well-known work on the Rinzai tradition, however, is certainly *The record of Linji*. Also called the *Linjilu*, or *Rinzai roku* in Japanese, it has been the essential text in Chinese and Japanese Zen Buddhism since the ninth century. There is an admirable translation and commentary on it by Ruth Fuller Sasaki, with a foreword by Yamada Mumon Roshi; the contents of the book were carefully edited by Thomas Yuho Kirchner, who also provided a deeply involving prologue (Sasaki, 2009). *The record of Linji* translates the *Discourses*, the *Critical Examination* and the *Record of Pilgrimages* of Rinzai. These are followed by an extensive and detailed *Commentary* by Sasaki. We can gain profound insights into

Rinzai from the recorded sayings of a Rinzai master, including a unique description of his life and teachings, his talks to audiences as well as numerous anecdotes and stories. The *Rinzai roku* provides the basic, fundamental tenets of the Rinzai teachings and tradition, the School of Sudden Enlightenment.

Trying to show this in a few words is inevitably hopeless; it can be better understood, however, by using the *Rinzai roku* as a sequence of koans to be studied with the master. What can be explored here is the direct approach to enlightenment which is shown in many different master's peculiar actions when addressing its disciples, including shouting and using a stick, the *keisaku*, to hit them. These actions, unexpected, unpredictable and sometimes incomprehensible, were popularised by the uniqueness of Zen teaching.

Realising the kensho is clearly the aim of devotees' training, yet at the same time, its essence is elusive. We can get an idea of the goal, however, from the Mumon's comment on Case 1 in the *Mumonkan*. The realisation of Zen understanding is represented by the success in passing through the barrier of the no-gate with a prolonged deep meditation on *Mu*. In Mumon's words, it will be just as swallowing a red-hot iron ball, which cannot be spat out until a sudden explosive conversion will occur. 'When you meet the Buddha, you kill him; when you meet the patriarchs, you kill them, enjoying a merry and playful samadhi' (Blyth, 1966; Sekida et al., 2005).

So far, we have explored past practices, mainly in Japan. Their description became available only in relatively recent times thanks to the indefatigable D.T. Suzuki's translations of traditional texts. First-hand experience of life and training in Zen monasteries were possible when Zen became an established presence in the United States at the beginning of the twentieth century and gained popularity after the Second World War. The Buddhist Society, London, was also actively involved in this process. This led some Americans to travel to Japan to experience entering a Zen monastery and receiving the same traditional training imparted reported in writings about Zen.

The difficulties foreigners encountered when travelling to Japan in the years immediately following the Second World War cannot be underestimated. The country was recovering from the devastation of the conflict and adopting a new constitution that would dramatically change its military traditions. Japan was forced to open to the outside world and faced a profound confrontation with Western culture, leading to dramatic social, economic and industrial changes.

Ruth Fuller Sasaki's writings are particularly valuable on this subject because of her first-hand deep experience of training and life in Ryosen-an at Daitokuji in Kyoto, as well as her experience with Western students training in a Japanese Zen monastery. In her book *Zen pioneer*, Sasaki describes her experience begun under the guidance of D.T. Suzuki and then continuing in Japan for the rest of her life; the chapter, *Accomplishment in Zen study*, explains her conclusions.

Sasaki had first-hand experience of the difficulty American students faced in finding accommodation and communicating with locals. Entry into a temple and adaptation to monastery life once admission was granted were also demanding. Studying Japanese, spoken and written, was unavoidable to allow at least some direct access to the texts used in koan studies, and for communicating with the Roshi during sanzen. Command of Japanese was helpful to develop interpersonal relationships with other monks. The study of ancient Chinese was additionally encouraged for direct access to the texts used for the training. It usually took at least one year to overcome these initial difficulties and to become sufficiently proficient at sitting in zazen for long periods without being distracted by aching legs, mental diversions and sleepiness. After this period, the Roshi had to decide whether the disciple could begin the real study of the koans. Many Japanese disciples stayed in the monastery for the shortest possible period, typically three years, but long enough for them to be recognised as abbots who could take charge of one of numerous temples across the country often one belonging to their family. The alternative was to decide to become a lay disciple, or take vows and devote themselves to becoming a fully ordained monk or priest. At the end of the first year, the students were able to involve themselves fully in the daily life of the monastery and study koans with the Roshi, which typically lasted one to three years. The few monks who were ambitious, talented and driven enough could then seek to become a recognised master, a Roshi, which involved remaining in the monastery for a period of 10 to 15 years, acquiring proficiency with the wide selection of Zen koans and commentaries, together with the elaborate ritual ceremonies expected from a Roshi (Sharf, 1995).

For those who did not drop out because of the hardship of the training or because they decided they would not find what they were looking for, a decision had to be made as to whether to continue training there or move elsewhere when a teacher was available, and once they had completed their initial practice. Sasaki then asks:

> After two or three years of practice, will the western student go home an enlightened man? That is a difficult question to answer. Undoubtedly he will have passed his first koan and perhaps some other koans as well. If he expects to have become what at present he conceives an enlightened man to be, then the answer is "No." But the man who returns will be a different man from the one who came. That I can promise. (Stirling, 2006)

Traditional Zen teachings have been thus passed down largely intact over the centuries, and the sequence of masters that transmitted the dharma seal, the *inka sonmei*, to their successors is preserved with devotion in temple lineages (Miura & Sasaki, 2015). This apparent consistency and homogeneity is not the whole story, however. There are some outstanding individuals who introduced remarkable innovations into their teachings, which sometimes were not transmitted to their successors. There are many examples in the anecdotes included in *Zen radicals, rebels and reformers* (Besserman & Steger, 2011): in the course of their lives, they made unexpected and extraordinary contributions to Zen. We have already encountered Rinzai, the reformer who shattered the formal rules of Zen. Ikkyu was an eccentric, iconoclastic Japanese Zen Buddhist monk and poet, who broke religious taboos including celibacy (Sanford, 1981). Bankei was a very popular figure, who has attracted many followers with his teachings based on the *unborn* as he called it, a simple and direct way to enlightenment (Bankei & Waddell, 2000). Hakuin is regarded as the reviver of the Rinzai School from a period of decay, through rigorous training grounded in the intense practice of koans (Waddell, 2010).

There are other noteworthy figures who contributed to the modernisation of Zen in the last century, such as Soen Nakagawa, a Taiwanese-born

Japanese Rinzai Roshi who had a substantial impact on Zen in Japan and abroad. There is also Nyoen Senzaki, who contributed significantly to the transmission of Zen to North America (Besserman & Steger, 2011).

So far, we have looked mainly at Zen traditions in Japan and not at the changes that have occurred over time. The state of Rinzai Zen in modern Japan is reported accurately and in great detail by Borup in *Japanese Rinzai Zen Buddhism Myōshinji, a living religion*. It focuses on the main Rinzai temple, Myoshinji, and goes from the institution, history and structure to the clergy, Dharma rank and hierarchy. The work also describes in detail the Zen religious education of both the priesthood and the laity, along with monastic practice. The modernisation and institutionalisation of lay and clerical rites are also considered (Borup, 2008).

Our main focus so far, both from explorations of the Japanese masters of the past and their successors, as well as Westerners who directly experienced Zen training and life in modern Japan, has largely been monastic life. It is therefore worth considering some other facets of Zen. It is not easy for Westerners to enter into direct contact with Japanese life and culture, past or present. The cultural differences between Japanese and Western culture are deeply rooted; they have been well evidenced by Doi in a small book which became a classic, *The anatomy of dependence: The key analysis of Japanese behaviour* (Doi, 1973).

There has historically been some limited contact between the laity and Zen masters and monks. Monasteries, temples and shrines are a conspicuous presence in Japan, and it was common to see monks during their periodic begging rounds, and their travel to other monasteries. Local populations were also actively involved in sustaining their community's temple, which they visited during ritual celebrations throughout the year, when they needed spiritual support for personal difficulties and for celebratory functions. Donations on these occasions, particularly from funerals, became one of the main incomes for the temples, alongside donations for other services the clergy provided the community. The clergy's services responded to individuals' spiritual needs, which were also often satisfied at home with small altars with the images of ancestors, which included a syncretism with aspects of Shintoism and other Buddhist traditions. The formal regular practice of meditation, however, and even less the practice of koan study, was not found outside monasteries. An issue thus arises: Zen Buddhism and Rinzai Zen are presented in many ways as the most direct path to enlightenment, yet their teachings are also the most difficult to grasp and put into practice for the general population, who do not have the necessary time, energy and detachment from daily life.

These same challenges arose when Zen Buddhism was brought outside Japan by the first pioneers who completed their full training as monks, in some cases also receiving the Dharma transmission from their Japanese Roshi, with the authorisation to act as a master themselves. The challenges of rigorous Zen practice for the wider population were replicated in the United States and Europe. Additionally, Western interest in Buddhism mainly centred on meditation, with limited consideration of the wider body of moral and doctrinal thought, in sharp contrast to Asia where the laity focused on moral precepts and rites, with limited interest in mediation.

In light of this, it seems that the lineage of Dharma transmission is in need of reconsideration. The tradition in Japan is that a Roshi at a traditional ancient monastery acknowledges the achievement of his disciple as the continuation of the line of past masters. In the West, after the arrival of the first Japanese-trained masters, transmission began to occur between their occidental disciples and their followers in contemporary temples newly founded in America and Europe.

There is a general need for modernisation, in both the West and the East, to make the practice of Zen more compatible with modern lay life. Some attempts were made in Japan by organisations such as the *F.A.S. Society* and *SamboKyodan*. These were attempts to combine the core of the teachings of the Soto and Rinzai Schools and the study of koans in a lay-friendly approach, which gained some popularity in the USA and Europe (Sharf, 1995). It seems that time, and the living adaptation and evolution of the core of Dharma teachings to modern global society may provide an answer to these challenging questions.

References

Anderson, J., & Schwartz, S. (2018). *Zen Odyssey the story of Sokei-an, Ruth Fuller Sasaki, and the birth of Zen in America*. Wisdom Publications.
Bankei, & Waddell, N. (2000). *The unborn: The life and teachings of Zen master Bankei, 1622–1693*. North Point Press.
Besserman, P., & Steger, M. B. (2011). *Zen radicals, rebels, and reformers*. Wisdom Publications.
Blyth, R. H. (1966). *Zen and Zen classics*. The Hokuseido Press.
Blyth, R. H. (1988). *Zen and Zen classics*. The Hokuseido Press.
Borup, J. (2008). *Japanese Rinzai Zen Buddhism: Myshinji, a living religion*. Brill.
Dōgen. (1988). Admonitions for Zazen. In *A complete English translation of dōgen Zenji's Shōbōgenzō (the eye and treasury of the true law)* (pp. 51–54). Distributed by Nakayama Shobō.
Doi, T. (1973). *The anatomy of dependence: The key analysis of Japanese behaviour*. Kodansha International.
Dumoulin, H. (1963). *A history of Zen Buddhism*. Faber.
Dumoulin, H., Heisig, J. W., & Knitter, P. (1990). *Zen Buddhism: A history*. Collier-Macmillan.
Giraldi, T. (2020). The spread of Buddhism from East to West. In *Psychotherapy, mindfulness and Buddhist meditation* (pp. 46–48). Palgrave Macmillan.
Gyatso, K. (1991). *The bodhisattva vow*. Tharpa.
Haynes, S. (2005). An exploration of Jack Kerouac's Buddhism: Text and life. *Contemporary Buddhism, 6*(2), 153–171. https://doi.org/10.1080/14639940500470031
Heine, S. (2004). Koans in the Dogen tradition: How and why Dogen does what he does with Koans. *Philosophy East and West, 54*(1), 1–19. https://doi.org/10.1353/pew.2003.0052
Hori Victor Sōgen. (2010). *Zen Sand: The book of capping phrases for Kōan practice*. University of Hawai'i Press.
Kapleau, P. (1967). *The three pillars of Zen: Teaching, practice and enlightenment*. Beacon Press.
Kirchner, T. Y. (2019). *Entangling vines: A classic collection of Zen koans*. Wisdom Publications.
Loori, J. D. (2012). *Sitting with koans: Essential writings on Zen Koan introspection*. Wisdom Publications.
Miles, B. (1989). *Ginsberg: A biography*. Simon and Schuster.

Miura, I., & Sasaki, R. F. (2015). *Zen dust: The history of the Koan and Koan study in Rinzai (Linji) Zen*. Melbourne University, VIC: Quirin Press.
O'Brien, B. (2019). *The circle of the way: A concise history of Zen from the Buddha to the modern world*. Shambhala.
Pasqualotto, G. (2003). *Il Buddhismo. I sentieri di una religione millenaria*. Bruno Mondadori.
Sanford, J. H. (1981). *Zen-Man Ikkyū*. Scholars Press.
Sasaki, R. F. (2009). *The record of Linji*. University of Hawaii Press.
Sekida, K., et al. (2005). *Two Zen classics: The gateless gate and the Blue Cliff Records*. Shambhala.
Sharf, R. (1995). Buddhist modernism and the rhetoric of meditative experience. *Numen, 42*(3), 228–283. https://doi.org/10.1163/1568527952598549
Snelling, J. (1999). *The Buddhist handbook*. Inner Traditions.
Snyder, G. (2014). *Nobody home: Writing, Buddhism, and living in places*. Trinity University Press.
Sogen, O. (2020). *Introduction to Zen training*. Tuttle Publishing.
Stirling, I. (2006). *Zen Pioneer: The life & works of Ruth Fuller Sasaki*. Shoemaker & Hoard.
Suzuki, D. T. (1934). *The training of the Zen Buddhist monk*. Eastern Buddhist Society.
Suzuki, D. T. (1964). *An introduction to Zen Buddhism*. Grove Press.
Suzuki, D. T. (1970). *Zen and Japanese culture*. Princeton University Press.
Suzuki, D. T., Fromm, E., & De Martino, R. (1960). *Zen Buddhism and psychoanalysis*. Harper.
Victor Sogen Hori. (2022). *Global Buddha*. Retrieved November 15, 2022, from http://globalbuddha.org/our-team/victor-sogen-hori/
Waddell, N. (1994). *Essential teachings of Zen master Hakuin*. Shambhala.
Waddell, N. (2010). *Wild ivy: The spiritual autobiography of Zen master Hakuin*. Shambhala.
Watts, A. (1962). *The way of Zen*. Penguin.
Wu, W. (2020). Temples and shrines of Japan—A brief guide. *Wendy Wu Asia Travel Inspiration*. Retrieved November 11, 2022, from https://www.wendywutours.com.au/blog/japans-temples-and-shrines-brief-guide/#:~:text=There%20are%20around%20100%2C000%20Shinto,from%20all%20over%20the%20world
Yamada, M., & Waddel, N. (2021). *Zen master Hakuin's song of zazen: Essays by Yamada Mumon rōshi*. Asia South Pacific Friendship Association.

4

Zen Moves West

After its birth in China, the Zen tradition spread to Asia, establishing itself in Japan, South-East Asia, Vietnam and Korea. Its core Buddhist and Zen teachings were preserved, however, as it established itself in a range of different forms in these cultures.

A unique and even iconoclastic outgrowth from mainstream Buddhism, Zen grew and flourished over the coming decades and centuries and even played a significant part in shaping Japanese culture.

Zen's common thread with mainstream Buddhism is the attainment of Buddhahood: enlightenment. Zen, however, emphasises this aspect over all others, offering a more direct path, stripped of the abstract concepts, the complex religious rituals of other Buddhist schools. In Japanese, Rinzai Zen, enlightenment or *kensho* and *satori*, must be sought through prolonged, deep meditation, zazen, as well as through the study of numerous koans. The Dharma transmission was passed down through an uninterrupted chain of masters, all of whom were formally recognised by their teacher through the *inka sonmei*, which in turn authorised them to pass on the Dharma teachings to their disciples. In the Soto School, by contrast, disciples sought gradual awakening, through prolonged periods of

T. Giraldi, *Zen Buddhism and the Reality of Suffering*,
https://doi.org/10.1007/978-3-031-69244-4_4

deep meditation in *samadhi*', *shikantaza*, the awakening or *shiho* being recognised by their master.

Soto and Rinzai monasteries have served several functions over time, all of which contributed to the preservation and continuity of their traditions. In some periods, however, large proportions of the populations of Rinzai monasteries were in fact simply staying there for shelter and to have a safe life in a respected institution. This became such a problem that Daito Kokushi (1283–1338), an influential master of the Rinzai school and founder of one of Kyoto's main temples, Daitokuji, decided to write the *Kozen Daito Kokushi Yuikai, Daito's Kokushi Admonitions.* This is a text which is still included in morning sutra chanting in Rinzai temples, and begins:

> All you monks who come to this mountain monastery, remember why you are assembled here: you have gathered for the practice of the Way, and not for food and clothing. While you have shoulders, you have clothes to wear, and while you have mouths, you have food to eat.

Daito Kokushi then continues asking the monks to follow a deep practice and warning them:

> Yet unless you truly dwell in your heart on the Wonderful Way that cannot be transmitted by Buddha and patriarchs, you will fail to bring forth the fruit and cause the downfall of the true line. (Myokyo-ni, 2008)

Particular emphasis was therefore placed on Dharma transmission as the confirmation of awakening by a teacher. It played an essential part in the continuation and maintenance of Zen institutions and was organised within an elaborate hierarchy of the main temples, their subsidiaries and sub-temples. There was also an analogous hierarchy of positions within each institution, where novices train to become priests and teachers of new novices.

Examining how Zen spread across the world, we must begin by tracing how the earliest forms of Buddhism, which form the core of Zen tradition, spread and established the early Schools of Buddhism.

The historic Buddha, Siddhartha Gautama, gave his original teachings during his 40 years travelling in Northern India in the fifth century BC. They were originally transmitted orally, and in spite of the lack of written source material, they spread widely and took root in many different parts of Asia. The Buddha's teachings were extremely broad and varied, and during their oral transmission to other Asian countries, they took on different ritual and canonical forms. It was soon realised that it was necessary to collect them as written texts, but this could not be achieved without serious difficulty. The first council to do this was held in the century after Siddhartha's death and was followed by three more in the following centuries before the birth of Christ. Even then, however, the leaders in attendance could not reach full agreement, and two more councils were held in the nineteenth century and then between 1954 and 1956 (Frasch, 2013).

It is important to note this in order to recognise the uniqueness of Buddhism. It is in effect a constellation of traditions which evolved independently from a central core of values that are strongly preserved, despite the heterogeneity of the traditions that sprung from them. Buddhism patently satisfied the spiritual needs of the societies in which it was practised, and in some instances, it formally became their national religion. Its non-theistic nature encourages peacefulness and strongly discourages any form of violence and even proselytising. Spreading from Northern India, traces of Hinduism can be detected in the later development of its traditional schools, including the concept of karma. When Buddhism moved into China, it was adapted to local Confucian values and also resonated particularly with the deepest values of Taoism. In Japan, Buddhism had no difficulty being adapted and integrated into Japan's native polytheistic and naturalistic Shinto culture.

Buddhism spontaneously spread not only to China and Japan but also to Tibet, Sri Lanka, Thailand, Korea, Myanmar and Vietnam, through the Mahayana, Hinayana and Vajrayana traditions. Zen would go on to follow a similar path, when it was introduced into China, later spreading and establishing local traditions in Buddhist countries such as Korea, Vietnam and Japan.

The introduction of Zen to Japan is attributed to the Patriarchs, whose followers established the three schools surviving today. In the thirteenth century, Dogen Zenji imported what is called the Soto School. The introduction of the Rinzai School is attributed to Myoan Eisai, while the third minor surviving sect, the Obaku, was established later by a small group of monks at the Manpukuji monastery during seventeenth century.

The Zen tradition has been maintained and transmitted through a network of temples and institutions, which grew in time to an astonishing size and consolidated the continuity of the schools and their traditions. Altogether, about 20,000 temples and 72 monasteries were erected mainly before and during the Tokugawa period, and most survive today (Bodiford, 1992).

During its long life in Japan, Zen progressively developed a stable and formal structure, which helped preserve it until the modern day. This is evidenced particularly by the large formal structure built around the values and traditions of Rinzai Zen, which is traced in great detail by Jorn Borup in his book *Japanese Rinzai Zen Buddhism: Myoshinji, a Living Religion* (Borup, 2008). Soto Zen also progressively developed a similarly organised structure, as had occurred with other Buddhist traditions such as Nichiren in the past, and in modern times, *Sanbo Kyodan*, *F.A.S. Society* and *Soka Gakkai* (Akizuki & Heisig, 1990; Kodo, 2004; Metraux, 1988).

At the same time as Zen traditions were developing and formalising in different parts of Japan, Zen followers began to encounter the same problems with preserving the original principles of Zen as outlined by Bodhidharma. In time, therefore, they began to establish monasteries far and wide, with their highly ritualised and organised monastic routines.

Dharma transmission, the formally certified authorisation to teach and pass on Dharma to select disciples, was central in establishing the lineages of masters and monasteries. Dharma teaching, however, encountered many difficulties in monastic life, so much so that one master of those times, Huineng, made profound reforms, particularly to the practice of koans that is central to the Rinzai tradition, which are still the basis for the training of Rinzai Zen monks today (Miura & Sasaki, 2015a, 2015b).

The study of koans, and the attainment of kensho, thus became the primary focus of the recognition of awakening by a teacher and played an essential part in the continuation and maintenance of Zen institutions, which were organised in elaborate hierarchies. Soto and Rinzai monasteries came to serve several different functions that helped preserve Zen traditions and, at the same time, profoundly influenced Japanese culture. It is worth noting, for example, the importance of funerals through the centuries in Japanese society, and the crucial role Zen monasteries, temples and priests play in providing ceremonial rites. Devotees also make substantial contributions to the survival and wealth of temples, particularly when funeral and other religious rites are provided (Bodiford, 1992).

Some of this has already been explored, and there are several accounts available of the traits Zen practice acquired in Japan. Zen training, and particularly its modern, living reality, has been described in detail (Ōmori et al., 2020; Hori, 1994); Zen monastic life is described in an excellent description by Nishimura (Nishimura & Smith, 1973).

It will be important, however, to bear these unique characteristics of Zen in mind when the meeting of Eastern and Western cultures and the spread of Buddhism in the West is considered. Western culture has been, and probably still is, largely Eurocentric, and it is noteworthy that for a long time, it paid remarkably little attention to the culture of the Eastern countries with which it came into contact through exploration, wars and trade. The oddity of this is doubly remarkable when considering that large parts of the planet, such as the Indian sub-continent as well as China, to name two examples, have ancient, rich and sophisticated cultural and religious histories, which were not accessed for a long time by Westerners, with the exception of a select few curious travellers and intellectuals.

Contact between East and West increased dramatically with the great voyages of exploration (and indeed, conquest) of the sixteenth century. The extensive exchanges that resulted were mainly focused on geopolitics and trade but unavoidably included some cultural and religious influence. The West's interest in the Asian religions and Buddhism, however, was initially limited (Wick & Rabens, 2014).

In fact, rather than exploring Asian faiths, Europeans focused more and more on converting populations to Christianity, and with the rise of the new colonial empires, this was increasingly accomplished through force. Acts of violence occurred during proselytising, religious wars were fought, and the Roman Catholic Inquisition often forced adherence. The impact would be long-lasting and can be seen today, for example, in the reach of Catholicism through almost all areas of Spanish influence, such as the South American continent and the archipelago of the Philippines.

In terms of the West's historic engagement with the monotheistic, Abrahamic religions, its encounters with the richness of Islamic culture have also most often involved wars of forced proselytising. Judaism often endured closer engagement and, in spite of its non-violent values, was subjected to perennial acts of persecution for its strict practices and cultural otherness. It is worth noting, in contrast, that at the same time, much of the Buddhist world was characterised by adherence to non-violence against sentient beings, and that the spread of the Buddhism to the countries where it took root occurred spontaneously without pressure for its adoption.

We have to wait until the later, colonial era, when European powers organised and stabilised their overseas domains, before we begin to see a significant widening of Western interest in Eastern cultures and religions. It is during this process that the West's interest in Buddhism began, grew and took new roots in remarkable and interesting ways.

Buddhism spread and developed a presence in the West, largely around the second half of the nineteenth century, because of several factors. The beginnings of global capitalism, which reached a new stage of complexity in this time, is one of the key factors. Immigration of people from distant places, on a scale never seen before, is another. When immigrants from Asia established themselves in North America, largely from China and Japan initially, their religious needs had to be satisfied and became known to native populations. At the same time, easier and faster travel and communications became available, allowing Western travellers to visit Asia more easily, along with Asian communities revisiting their place of origin; this, too, was a factor. The intellectual knowledge of Buddhism thus grew and was enriched by its practice when Western visitors established themselves in Buddhist countries and came into direct contact with Buddhist practices.

Western systematic and organised interest in Zen also began towards the end of the nineteenth century. This was a largely spontaneous process, when Zen's unique characteristics were encountered by curious and open-minded pioneers. It was a fruitful and successful process, in spite, and perhaps also because, of the extreme differences between the deeply ingrained existential and cultural values of the newly converted Westerners, and those of the Asian cultures where Zen had developed.

Rick Fields' revised and updated *How the Swans Came to the Lake* (Fields & Bogin, 2022) is a rich source of information about the establishment of Buddhism in the West. It is clearly most interested in events in America but provides at the same time a detailed account of what happened outside America because of the interconnectedness of the whole picture. A shorter description of the Asian origins of Buddhism, its spread to the West and views about its future can also be found in James Coleman's *New Buddhism* (Coleman, 2002).

The World's Columbian Exposition, also known as the Chicago World's Fair, was held in Chicago in 1893 to celebrate the 400th anniversary of Christopher Columbus' arrival in the New World in 1492. This was also the occasion when the Parliament of World Religions was organised for the first time, in an attempt to create a global dialogue of faiths. The representatives were overwhelmingly Christians of various denominations, but alongside them were also representatives from other religions, such as the Sri Lankan Buddhist leader Anagarika Dharmapala, who was invited as a representative of Southern Buddhism, the term applied at that time to Theravada. For Zen Buddhism, which soon will put down roots in North America, the representatives included a number of people who would have a substantial influence on the future of Zen in the West.

Soyen Shaku, the First American Ancestor of Zen, attended from Japan and returned to the United States in 1905, at the invitation of a wealthy couple, Alexander and Ida Russell. He established a small zendo near San Francisco, thus becoming the first Zen Buddhist priest to teach in America.

Daisetz Teitaro Suzuki was also present because of his close connection to Soyen Shaku, his master. Soyen Saku suggested to Paul Carus that Suzuki could help with the translation and publishing of Eastern spiritual literature in the West, both because of his direct knowledge of the practice of Zen and his good command of the English language (Meyer, 1962). This was the beginning of a prolonged and productive literary life, which led him to be recognised as a sort of representative ambassador of Zen Buddhism, especially during the later part of his long life which ended in 1966 (Cunningham, 2020). His works give a unique view of the extremely wide corpus of texts, previously inaccessible to Western scholars and devotees. Because of his first-hand experience as a pupil of his roshi teacher together with his wide scholarly knowledge, he was able to provide unique and universally acknowledged contributions. He was also, however, a child of his time, and some critiques have recently been made of the way in which he depicted Zen (Fader, 1980); his works nevertheless remain relevant. This comes across clearly in the works of the other people who enabled the diffusion of Zen in America and beyond, such as Christmas Humphreys, Thomas Merton, Eric Fromm, Alan Watts, Philip Kapleau, Gary Snider and Robert Aitken (Haar & Abe, 1986).

The dissemination of Zen throughout the United States also continued both alongside Shaku's presence beginning in 1906 and after, with his disciple Shigetsu Sasaki (monastic name Sokei-an), who took up permanent residence in the USA. After years of peregrination on the West Coast and after completing his training and ordination in Japan, he moved to New York City at the beginning of the 1930s to establish a group that was later named *The First Zen Institute of America*, and which is still active today.

From the beginning, Ruth Fuller Everett was an active presence. She had an exceptional personality and remarkable wealth and contributed significantly to the establishment of the *Zen Institute* in New York. Shortly before the death of Sokei-an in 1945, he and Ruth would marry, and she took the name of Ruth Fuller Sasaki. Her outstanding contributions continued, and after 1949, she began establishing herself in Kyoto, Japan, where she spent most of the rest of her life. She became in 1958 the first foreigner, Westerner and the only woman, to be an ordained priest of Daitokuji, one of the main Rinzai Zen temples in Kyoto. She was then able to step up her activities and became instrumental in enabling American students to reside in Kyoto to undergo Zen training (which would have otherwise been impossible in those times). Her story and the role she played, together with Sokei-an Sasaki, in establishing Zen in America, are clearly portrayed in her biography *Zen Pioneer: The Life & Works of Ruth Fuller Sasaki* (Stirling, 2006) and in *Zen Odyssey. The story of Sokei-an, Ruth Fuller Sasaki, and the Birth of Zen in America* (Anderson

& Schwartz, 2018). Ruth Sasaki has also been involved in making an extremely accurate, detailed English translation of the classic text *The Record of Linji, The Sayings of Master Rinzai* (Sasaki & Kirchner, 2009), and also *Zen Dust; the History of the Koan and Koan Study in Rinzai (Linchi) Zen* (Miura & Sasaki, 2015a, 2015b).

Around these central figures were also other characters who were crucial for the spread of Zen to the West. Ruth Fuller Sasaki was the mother-in-law of Alan Watts, who later contributed significantly to the popularisation of Zen in America (Watts, 1973). Earlier on, in 1911, Daisetz Suzuki was married to Beatrice Erskine Lane, an outstanding woman who is central in the introduction of Theosophy to Japan. She was educated at Radcliffe College, from which she graduated in 1898 and where one of her tutors was William James, one of the most influential philosophers of the United States at the time, who is considered the 'father' of American psychology (Allen, 1967; Algeo, 2007).

The theme of Theosophy deserves some consideration, particularly because of its unique history and the role it played in attracting the interest in Eastern mysticism and faiths in the West. Indeed, at the First Parliament of the World's Religions, the Vice President of the Theosophical Society, William Quan Judge, was present alongside the representatives of many and varied Asian religions and cults including Zen, and the activist Annie Besant.

Theosophy is a movement which was established in New York City in 1875 by Helena Blavatsky, Henry Olcott and William Quan Judge. It is largely based on Blavatsky's writings, and is categorised by scholars of the subject as a sort of new religious movement, whose origins can be traced to Western esotericism and occultism, older European philosophies and Asian religions such as Hinduism and Buddhism. It is almost unbelievable how Blavatsky, herself self-educated, organised in an ingenious and rather naïve and captivating way, a whole system which she claimed was based on the teachings of ancient masters and religions. A brotherhood was also established, based on a complex system of initiations, which formed part of the hierarchy of an entire, new cosmological system. Blavatsky described her theories in two books, *Isis Unveiled* (Blavatsky, 2022) and *The Secret Doctrine* (Blavatsky, 2019) which she wrote while she travelled in various Eastern countries, also in the company of Olcott, with whom she later relocated to India.

Theosophy contributed to the wealth of its founders through donation requests to new initiates as they entered the organisation and progressed through its hierarchy. Since its beginning, Theosophy has been criticised as a smart invention without any serious foundations. Krisnamurti gives a clear account of its contradictions and extravagancies, based on his training from an early age in the complex workings of the organisation, though he later distanced himself from it (Lutyens, 1990). Among the critiques raised against Theosophy, an early example is *The Fraud of Modern "Theosophy" Exposed: A Brief History of the Greatest Imposture Ever Perpetrated Under the Cloak of Religion* (Maskelyne & Price, 2014); one of the latest is *Against Blavatsky: Rene Guenon's Critique of Theosophy* (Smoley, 2010). Somewhat surprisingly, Theosophy still survives today, maintaining an international following. It is worth considering the case of Theosophy in connection with the universal human need for religion and faith, and in the case of the 'cargo cults', which exemplify the difficulty of identifying the boundary between good faith and deliberate fraud and plagiarism in new religious movements.

It was from this world that Western interest in Buddhism, and especially Zen, began to grow and flourished between 1950 and 1975. The popularity of Zen in these years is largely associated with the success of books by Reginal Horace Blyth, Alan Watts and Philip Kapleau. In the same years, Zen also caught the attention of Beat poets such as Jack Kerouac, Allen Ginsberg and Gary Snyder. Its popularity grew substantially after the literary magazine *The Chicago Review* published a special issue on Zen in 1958 whose contributors included, together with Kerouac and Snyder, Alan Watts, Daisetz Teitaro Suzuki and Ruth Fuller Sasaki (Chicago Review. On Zen, 1958). It was not long after this that Eric Fromm together with Daisetz Teitaro Suzuki also published *Zen Buddhism and Psychoanalysis* (Fromm & Suzuki, 1970). Interest in this book came particularly from the popularity of its authors, especially Fromm, and it reached an even larger audience with the Carl Jung's *Foreword to Suzuki's Introduction to Zen Buddhism* (Suzuki, 1964; Jung, 1978).

These people and their initiatives were the seeds for the organisation of the first stable, long-standing Zen institutions in America after the *Zen*

Institute in New York. In California, Taizan Maezumi and Shunryu Suzuki helped to establish the Soto Zen sect and inspired the foundation of the *Zen Center* in Los Angels and *San Francisco Zen Center*. *Zen Mind, Beginner's Mind,* the book of the teachings of Suzuki, became one of the most-read books on Zen and Buddhism, significantly contributing to the popularisation of Zen in the West (Chadwick, 1999; Suzuki & Dixon, 2020).

There were other initiatives headed by Japanese masters, however, such as the foundation of the *Mount Baldy Zen Center* in California by Kyozan Joshu Sasaki, one of the most influential Zen masters in America. Eido Tai Shimano contributed to the foundation of the *New York Zendo Shoboji,* and *Dai Bosatsu Zendo Kongoji* monastery in the Catskill Mountains of New York.

Meanwhile, in Honolulu, Omori Sogen Roshi founded *Daihonzan Chozenji,* the first fully recognised Rinzai temple outside Japan (Seager, 2012). There is a full account of these events, along with more general analysis of the global rise of Buddhism in Baumann's book on the subject (Baumann, 2001).

From its roots in China, Zen firmly established itself first in Japan, Korea and Vietnam and these local traditions also spread to the West. This happened for Korean *Seon Zen* thanks to the work of Seung Sahn and Samu Sanim, and by their followers, who founded a series of centres in the United States and other Western countries (Park, 2010).

Vietnamese *Thien Zen* became popular in the West, thanks to the work of Thich Nath Hanh, a monk, peace activist, prolific author and teacher. A recognised Zen teacher, Thich Nath Hanh opened the practice to the modern West by giving his followers an easily accessible presentation of Zen practice, yet still remaining strictly within Buddhist teachings and traditions. Along with his forthright teachings, he also published a large number of articles and books and raised the banner of peace internationally. He founded the *Order of Interbeing* as a new modernist and humanistic form of Vietnamese Zen, promoting the idea of a unified Buddhism. To this end, he also founded the *Plum Village* tradition in the United States, which has also gained a presence in France. He was, in this sense, a precursor of the Western mindfulness phenomenon that gained such traction at the end of the 1990s, presenting it, however, in a pure Buddhist form, with strict adherence to the main Mahayana and Hinayana teachings and texts (Hạnh, 2019).

These are some of the key figures who, through their initiatives, planted the first seeds of Zen in the United States. Following their personal paths, they came into contact with the world and practice of Zen under the guidance of Japanese roshi, recognised by Japanese Zen institutions. The first generation of Westerners who led the popularisation of Zen in the West were disciples of recognised Japanese masters. Some were destined to play a special role in the continuation of traditional Zen in the West, becoming lay monks or even priests, through the Dharma transmission.

Alan Watts deserves special mention here for his prolific work as a writer and populariser in America. One additional reason to cite him is that he is an example of the interconnectedness of the figures in this story. Indeed, Watts was born and educated in England, where he became acquainted with the *Buddhist Lodge*, which later became the *Buddhist Society* in London, both founded by Christmas Humphreys; through these contacts, he also became acquainted with Daisetz Teitaro Suzuki. After establishing himself in America, where he spent a large part of his life, he also married the mother of Ruth Fuller Sasaki, Eleanor Everett. He also played a key part in drawing a connection between the Zen path and research into consciousness, psychedelics, mental health and psychotherapy (Furlong, 1987; Watts, 1963, 1973).

There are numerous other figures in the diffusion of Zen in the West, many of whom are portrayed by James Ishmael Ford in his book *Zen Master Who* (Ford, 2006). There are two people in particular whom it is important to mention, and whose contributions help showing some of the problems that arose in translating Zen from its original Buddhist framework in Asia, to the radically different cultures of Europe and America. Robert Aitken lived a rich life, with long sojourns in the United States, spending a large part of his life in Hawaii. He was deeply involved in the problems of social injustices and is one of the founders of the Buddhist Peace Fellowship. He met and began his practice with several Japanese Zen masters, such as Hakuun Yasutani. Along with Eido Tai Shimano, he also established the *Diamond Sangha Centre* in Honolulu. He became a disciple of Koun Yamada, receiving permission to teach and

Dharma transmission, formally becoming a Roshi in the Harada Yashutani lineage (Fields & Bogin, 2022; Seager, 2012).

Philip Kapleau spent a long and productive life mainly in America, founding in 1966 the *Rochester Zen Center* where he taught for the rest of his life. His main teacher was Hakuun Yasutani, with whom he completed a large part of the traditional koan curriculum of the Rinzai tradition, then obtaining authorisation to teach. He did not receive Dharma transmission, however, and distanced himself from previous teachers, starting his own Zen lineage and creating his own Dharma transmission, which he passed on to several disciples around the world. His teachings differed substantially from previous Zen schools, and he formed the *SanboKyodan* tradition, a sort of blend of Soto and Rinzai doctrines, aimed to be more appropriate for modern times and Western society (Ford, 2006; Sharf, 1995a, 1995b). His views were described in a book, *The Three Pillars of Zen*, which reached a large audience in America and abroad (Kraft, 2000).

While these events were occurring mainly in America, Buddhism and Zen also spread substantially in Europe (Baumann, 2015; Borup, 2021). On this issue, it is worth looking at the role played by Christmas Humphreys, who worked relentlessly to bring Buddhism to the West. His work was wide-ranging and is quite difficult to summarise it in a limited space. Suffice it to say that he was initially involved with Theosophy, which he later abandoned, founding in 1924 the London Buddhist Lodge, which was renamed as the Buddhist Society, and which still exists today as one of the oldest Buddhist organisations outside Asia with Western founders. He was instrumental in bringing a range of spiritual and intellectual authorities into the orbit of the society, including for Zen Daisetz Teitaro Suzuki and Alan Watts, whom we have already met. With time, the society became a centre for the practice and study of the Hinayana, Mahayana and Vajrayana traditions (Humphreys, 1978).

As far as Zen is concerned, Humphreys also brought the society into connection with Irmgard Schlögl, who had the Dharma name of *Myokyo-Ni*. An Austrian geologist, she joined the Zen Group at the Buddhist Society under Christmas Humphreys in 1950. From 1960, she undertook a long period of training in Japan at Daitokuji monastery, after which she returned to England in 1972, to live with Humphreys as part of the formal Zen group he had established at his home. After his death, it became *Shobo-an, Hermitage of the True Dharma*, a residential Rinzai Zen training temple. Myokyo-ni was formally ordained, and Shobo-an was recognised as a temple associated with Daitokuji in 1984. *Fairlight* in Luton, the second of the Buddhist Society's two training temples, is similarly recognised, and both are active under the guidance of Schlögl's disciples (Blomfield, 2007).

It is also appropriate to note the work of Taisen Deshimaru in establishing Soto Zen in Europe. Deshimaru lived a large part of his life in Japan, though not in a Zen temple. He gained a large following in France, where he later set up residence and taught Soto Zen. There were, however, controversies because of his lack of recognition as a master by Japanese Zen institutions. Nevertheless, he had a large number of followers and pupils, who continued his teachings in Europe after his death; they were active in keeping and developing connections with Japan, which were formally re-established, and played a significant role in creating a Europe-wide Soto Zen organisation.

When we consider how Zen spread to the West, we must take a number of factors into account, all mutually interacting and contributing to a complex and dynamic picture. This analysis, difficult by itself, is rendered even more complex by the profound difference between Japanese, American and European cultures. Historically, Japanese contact with the West had been markedly limited. Moreover, the Japanese have a sort of traditional diffidence towards Westerners, who as foreigners are collectively grouped under the term *gaijin*, which are believed to be largely incapable of understanding the subtleties of Japanese mores, characterised by '*amae*' in a classic analysis by Takeo Doi (Doi, 1973). This has to be kept in mind, when considering the spread of Zen outside Japan.

We already saw that Zen in Japan was based on a large network of temples and sub-temples, with a strict hierarchy and administrative organisation. There is a vast network for the Soto School, with the head temples of Eiheiji and Sojiji, along with a large number of smaller sub-temples. Rinzai has its historical and traditional temples in Kyoto, such as Myoshinji, Daitokuji and Tenryuji, which were founded by some of the great masters of the past. A large number of smaller temples also exist across the country, together with sub-temples specialising in the training of Western monks, such as Shofukuji in Kobe. Most of the smaller shrines around the country serve mainly as a local religious presence and for religious services (Bodiford, 1993; Borup, 2008). Buddhist universities are also associated with the main temples, like the Komazawa University for Soto and the Hanazono University for Rinzai Zen.

This was the state of Zen as the curious and courageous few would have discovered it with its exotic and puzzling features challenging a Western mind. There had already been some encounters, mainly at an intellectual and cultural level, when some British intellectuals came into contact with Buddhist scriptures and monks in places under British colonial rule. A significant contribution in this area was from Edward Conze and Reginald Horace Blyth, adding to the work by Daisetz Teitaro Suzuki (Garofalo, 2017; Sangharakshita, 1996).

The real experience of Zen, as it was practised by Japanese monks, however, was only encountered by the very few who were motivated enough to move to Japan. This happened mainly after the Second World War when American soldiers came into contact with the Far East.

The reality of Zen at this time was that there were temples founded centuries before, where the same rituals had been strictly preserved and followed. The temple was run under the authority of the resident master, and everything happening there was strictly focused on the achievement of awakening, the enlightenment common to all Buddhist teachings and scriptures.

This, together with the various writings and illustrations which became available in the early part of the twentieth century, may help to understand how the world of Japanese Zen attracted the modern American mind. Understanding of Zen, however, unavoidably came through the experiences of those Westerners who had already decided to approach it, and it is crucial to recognise how different this experience would be to that of a person who was born and had grown up in Japan. The difficulties arising from this difference soon became clear.

Those who entered Japanese temples had to overcome formidable challenges. These include a basic resistance to accepting foreigners into traditional teaching temples, the need to have a good command of Japanese in order to adequately live the daily routine, to understand the master's teachings and to have sufficient social interactions within and outside the temple. Behind these initial difficulties, there was also the inherent challenge of the practice. For Rinzai Zen, the time from initiation to the first experience of *kensho* might be approximately three to five years. And that was just the beginning of the practice of koans in the lineage's particular curriculum, with the total number which would be in the hundreds. Completing this path could usually take 20 or more years. This was the experience of some of those who decided to train in Japan and were later fully recognised as masters, for example, Ruth Fuller Sasaki and Myokyo-ni. Some, such as Thomas Yuho Kirchner and Jeff Shore, completed their koan training and decided to stay in Japan as teachers at Hanazono University and its attached Institute for Zen Studies and the International Research Institute for Zen Buddhism, producing valuable written works (Myokyo-ni, 2008; Shore, 1996; Sharf, 1995a, 1995b; Stirling, 2006).

Zen was thus brought to the West by the pupils of traditional Japanese training temples, as well as by disciples who encountered their Japanese masters in the USA. This complicated the meaning of the Dharma transmission and the Zen training path. Teachers who had lived within the strict and impersonal routines of a Zen temple organised according to ancient Japanese traditions, soon found themselves confronted by the realities of American contemporary society and the centres where live teaching took place.

The Zen masters of the past have been represented in many books in an undoubtedly hagiographic and even mystical manner. Anecdotes about their lives and relationships with their pupils present them as having unquestioned authority and knowledge, without any doubt as to their actual enlightenment. Masters were the guides for their disciples, working to provide the monks in training with the ideal conditions for *kensho* through the routine of temple life.

The largely idealised figure of the Japanese monk master, who would often have spent large parts of their life in a Zen monastery, had to be adapted to the realities of a completely different life in America. The cultural background of their disciples, radically different from those of religious and lay followers in Japan, was an additional challenge. The core of the traditional Zen teachings by a Japanese roshi available to wider American society caused a greater degree of scrutiny for the basic principles behind the authority and structure of Zen traditions. As this rhetoric was accessed by American audiences, a series of questions were raised. What is the nature and reality of awakening through kensho and satori? What is the reality of the Dharma transmission? What is the inka and how does it confirm that kensho and satori were authentic, and part of a specific lineage? The curious Western minds began to question the relationship between individual awakening and appointment as a roshi or head of a temple, the strictness of the hierarchy of Zen temples and institutions, the nature of the master-pupil relationship and the influence it could have on the personal life of a disciple. The figure of the master could now be observed not only within the routines of a temple but outside, in the context of contemporary daily Western life. American men and women started to question the potential conflicts between their lives and their new Buddhist faith, together with the sometimes authoritarian demands of the masters.

The credibility and respectability of Buddhism in the West suffered in some instances the blows of a series of sex scandals involving the Tibetan *Shambala* and *Rigpa Organisation* (Bell, 2019; Newman, 2018; Shute, 2018). Zen also suffered embarrassing episodes, including the example of the *San Francisco Zen Centre*, founded by Suzuki Roshi and later run by his follower Richard Baker: their behaviour with female disciples and the difficulties in their family life were found to be far from what was expected from a roshi.

Different problems arose in the case of Philip Kapleau. After allegedly completing the traditional koan curriculum given by his teachers and in particular Yasutani Roshi, his Dharma transmission was never formally acknowledged nor was he included in the lineage of his master; nevertheless, he still persisted in imparting his own teachings.

There are several other allegations of serious misconduct and ensuing scandals, which involved the generation of Japanese masters who introduced Zen to the United States in the period following the Second World War.

Eido Shimano Roshi, the pupil of Soen Nakagawa, was implicated in sex scandals involving the harassment of female disciples. This became known outside the Zen centres where he was master and forced him to formally resign from his role. Joshu Sasaki Roshi was the master at Mt.

Baldy Zen Center in California, where the popular singer Leonard Cohen practised, resided and was ordained. In the last years of his life, a scandal emerged involving a long series of improper sexual acts with his disciples and nuns. One final case is that of Taizan Mazumi Roshi, who was involved in a widely publicised sex scandal.

There is a wide selection of works dedicated to better understanding Zen Buddhism on *Zen Buddhism WWW Virtual Library* (Ciolek & Keremidschieff, 2023), where the facts mentioned above are laid out in detail. Stuart Lachs has also published *Zen Essays: Critical Zen*, a series of works exploring the contrast between the reality of the behaviour of Zen masters and the hagiographic works published about them. Their titles include: *Means of Authorization: Establishing Hierarchy in Ch'an/Zen Buddhism in America* (Lachs, 2006a), *Richard Baker and the Myth of the Zen Roshi* (Lachs, 2002), *When the Saints Go Marching In: Modern Day Zen Hagiography* (Lachs, 2011) and *The Zen Master in America: Dressing the Donkey with Bells and Scarves* (Lachs, 2006b).

The picture which emerges is that of a strong tradition, deeply ingrained with Japanese culture, based on a large number of temples and institutions, which carefully preserves the traditions of the Soto and Rinzai schools, but which became complicated when translated from Japan to America and other Western countries. There, the original values of these traditions are confronted with the challenges of adaptation to a modern Western society.

New difficulties also emerged for the Western Zen tradition, which can be summarised under the titles of sustainability, legitimacy and authority. The concepts of Dharma transmission and lineage had to be reconsidered, and new attempts had to be made to reorder a disoriented world, laying the grounds for continuity and recognition by the original Japanese institutions. The American Zen Teachers Association is an example of the work to establish rules of conduct and uniformity in the Zen centres across the country (Koné, 2015; Heine & Wright, 2010).

Whole new themes thus appeared that update the characteristics of traditional Buddhist Zen, which had survived and continues to survive after centuries in Japan. And it is that with these new characteristics, it established his new roots in the West.

It is difficult to trace precisely how the basic values of Zen, initially defined by Bodhidharma, have been retained not only in Japan but also outside it. This, indeed, was the challenge raised by Daito Koukushi in his *Admonitions,* which are a reminder to the followers of the Way of the need to preserve and transmit *the mysterious and un-transmissible Way of the Buddhas and of Patriarchs* in its essential form. The need for reform, particularly in the training of Buddhist monks, was felt and addressed centuries later by people such as Hakuin Ekaku. More recently, however, more efforts have been made to modernise Buddhism and Zen, in Japan and in the West, to make it more accessible and practicable in contemporary Eastern and Western society.

In Japan, Zen has a strong grounding in its traditional temples and institutions that guarantee the continuity at least of its formal practice. The same dynamic evolution which occurred in the past may continue in the future, with new challenges and unexpected novelties only resolved with time. Yamada Mumon Roshi, a Zen master whom some consider the last of the great traditional Rinzai Zen masters, was interviewed about the future of Zen in 1977 by Ronald Eyre for the BBC series *Buddhism: The Land of the Disappearing Buddha, Japan* about his previous statement 'Zen in Japan is dead, and ought to be re-imported from America' answering with a delightful and enigmatic smile (Eyre, 2016).

Whatever the various traditions in the practice of Zen and Buddhism are themes which remain crucial, deserving deeper consideration, and enlightenment, the awakening is certainly one of them. Besides its relevance for Dharma transmission and the lineage, this is one of the core aspects of Zen, which attracted the interest of psychology, and will be examined in more detail in the next chapter.

References

Akizuki, R., & Heisig, J. W. (1990). *New Mahāyāna: Buddhism for a post-modern world*. Asian Humanities Press.

Algeo, A. S. (2007). Beatrice Lane Suzuki: An American theosophist in Japan. *Quest, 95*(1), 13–17.

Allen, G. W. (1967). *William James: A biography*. Viking.

Anderson, J., & Schwartz, S. (2018). *Zen Odyssey. The story of Sokei-an, Ruth Fuller Sasaki, and the birth of zen in America*. Wisdom Publications.

Baumann, M. (2001). Global Buddhism: Developmental periods, regional histories, and a new analytical perspective. *Journal of Global Buddhism, 2*, 1–43. https://doi.org/10.5281/zenodo.1310640

Baumann, M. (2015). Global Buddhism: Developmental periods, regional histories, and a new analytical perspective. *Journal of Global Buddhism, 2*, 1–43. https://doi.org/10.5281/zenodo.1310640

Bell, S. (2019). 15 scandals in emerging Western Buddhism. *Westward Dharma*, 230–242. https://doi.org/10.1525/9780520936584-016

Blavatsky, H. P. (2019). *The Secret Doctrine*. Retrieved March 29, 2023, from https://www.theosociety.org/pasadena/sd/sd-hp.htm

Blavatsky. (2022). ISIS unveiled, volume 1 (of 2), science by H. P. Blavatsky. *Project Gutenberg*. Retrieved March 29, 2023, from https://www.gutenberg.org/ebooks/68705

Blomfield, S. (2007). Obituary: The venerable Myokyo-ni. *The Guardian*. Retrieved April 30, 2023, from https://www.theguardian.com/news/2007/apr/23/guardianobituaries.religion

Bodiford, W. M. (1992). Zen in the art of funerals: Ritual salvation in Japanese Buddhism. *History of Religions, 32*(2), 146–164. https://doi.org/10.1086/463322

Bodiford, W. M. (1993). *Soto Zen in medieval Japan*. University of Hawaii Press.

Borup, J. (2008). *Japanese Rinzai Zen Buddhism: MyŌshinji, a living religion*. Brill.

Borup, J. (2021). Introduction. Japanese Buddhism in Europe. *Journal of Religion in Japan, 10*(2–3), 113–133. https://doi.org/10.1163/22118349-01002010

Chadwick, D. (1999). *Crooked cucumber: The life and Zen teaching of Shunryu Suzuki*. Thorsons.

Chicago Review. 'On Zen'. (1958). JSTOR *Chicago Review* (Vol. 12, No. 2, Summer, 1958). Retrieved from https://www.jstor.org/stable/i25293446

Ciolek, M. D. T. C., & Keremidschieff, V. (2023). *Zen Buddhism WWW Virtual Library, Asia Pacific Research Online*. Retrieved May 12, 2023, from http://www.ciolek.com/WWWVL-Zen.html

Coleman, J. W. (2002). *The new Buddhism: The western transformation of an ancient tradition*. Oxford University Press.

Cunningham, E. (2020). D. T. Suzuki: A biographical summary. *Association for Asian Studies*. Retrieved March 27, 2023, from https://www.asianstudies.org/publications/eaa/archives/d-t-suzuki-a-biographical-summary/

Doi, T. (1973). *The anatomy of dependence: The key analysis of Japanese behaviour*. Kodansha International.

Eyre, R. (2016). *A documentary of Zen Buddhism in Japan*. YouTube. Retrieved May 15, 2023, from https://www.youtube.com/watch?v=WUsC3f4Dqxk&t=2466s

Fader, L. A. (1980). Arthur Koestler's critique of D. T. Suzuki's interpretation of Zen. *The Eastern Buddhist, 13*(2), 46–72.

Fields, R., & Bogin, B. (2022). *How the Swans came to the lake: A narrative history of Buddhism in America*. Shambhala Publications, Inc.

Ford, J. I. (2006). *Zen master who?: A guide to the people and stories of Zen*. Wisdom Publications.

Frasch, T. (2013). Buddhist councils in a time of transition: Globalism, modernity and the preservation of textual traditions. *Contemporary Buddhism, 14*(1), 38–51. https://doi.org/10.1080/14639947.2013.785245

Fromm, E., & Suzuki, D. T. (1970). *Zen Buddhism and psychoanalysis*. Harper and Row.

Furlong, M. (1987). *Genuine fake: A biography of Alan Watts*. Unwin Paperbacks.

Garofalo, M. P. (2017). *Blyth, Reginald Horace; (1898–1964)*. Retrieved May 5, 2023, from https://www.gardendigest.com/zen/blyth.htm

Haar, F., & Abe, M. (1986). *A Zen life: D.T. Suzuki remembered*. Weatherhill.

Hạnh, N. (2019). *At home in the World: Stories and essential teachings from a monk's life*. Parallax Press.

Heine, S., & Wright, D. S. (2010). *Zen masters*. Oxford University Press.

Hori, G. V. (1994). Teaching and learning in the Rinzai Zen Monastery. *Journal of Japanese Studies, 20*(1), 5. https://doi.org/10.2307/132782

Humphreys, C. (1978). *Both sides of the circle: The autobiography*. Allen & Unwin.

Jung, C. (1978). Foreword to Suzuki's "Introduction to Zen Buddhism". In *Psychology and the East* (pp. 138–157). Princeton University Press.

Kodo, M. (2004). *A guide to Japanese Buddhism*. Retrieved March 20, 2023, from http://www.buddhanet.net/pdf_file/guidejapanbuddhismbm6.pdf

Koné, A. (2015). Zen in Europe: A survey of the Terristory. *Journal of Global Buddhism, 2*, 139–161. https://doi.org/10.5281/zenodo.1310681

Kraft, K. (2000). *Zen teaching, Zen practice: Philip Kapleau and the three pillars of Zen*. Weatherhill.

Lachs, S. (2002). Richard Baker and the myth of the Zen roshi. *thezensite*. Retrieved May 12, 2023, from http://www.thezensite.com/ZenEssays/CriticalZen/Richard_Baker_and_the_Myth.htm

Lachs, S. (2006a). Means of authorization: Establishing hierarchy. In *Ch'AN/Zen Buddhism in America, thezensite*. Retrieved May 12, 2023, from http://www.thezensite.com/ZenEssays/CriticalZen/Means_of_Authorization.htm

Lachs, S. (2006b). The Zen master in America: Dressing the donkey with bells and scarves. *thezensite*. Retrieved May 12, 2023, from https://www.thezensite.com/ZenEssays/CriticalZen/Zen_Master_in_America.html

Lachs, S. (2011). When the Saints Go Marching in: Modern day Zen hagiography... *thezensite*. Retrieved May 12, 2023, from https://www.thezensite.com/ZenEssays/CriticalZen/When_the_Saints_Go_Marching_Marching_In.pdf

Lutyens, M. (1990). *The life and death of Krisnamurti*. Rider.

Maskelyne, J. N., & Price, H. (2014). *The fraud of modern 'Theosophy' exposed: A brief history of the greatest imposture ever perpetrated under the cloak of religion*. Routledge.

Metraux, D. A. (1988). *The history and theology of Soka Gakkai: A Japanese new religion*. E. Mellen.

Meyer, D. H. (1962). Paul Carus and the religion of science. *American Quarterly, 14*(4), 597. https://doi.org/10.2307/2710135

Miura, I., & Sasaki, R. F. (2015a). The history of the Koan in Rinzai (Linji) Zen. In *Zen dust: The history of the Koan and Koan study in Rinzai (Linji) Zen* (pp. 3–30). Melbourne University, VIC: Quirin Press.

Miura, I., & Sasaki, R. F. (2015b). *Zen dust: The history of the Koan and Koan study in Rinzai (Linji) Zen*. Melbourne University, VIC: Quirin Press.

Myokyo-ni. (Ed.). (2008). National Teacher Daito on his deathbed admonishes his monks. In *The daily devotional chants of the Zen Centre* (pp. 84–85). The Buddhist Society.

Newman, A. (2018). The 'king' of Shambhala Buddhism is undone by abuse report. *The New York Times*. Retrieved May 11, 2023, from https://www.nytimes.com/2018/07/11/nyregion/shambhala-sexual-misconduct.html

Nishimura, E., & Smith, B. L. (1973). *Unsui: A diary of Zen monastic life*. University Press of Hawaii.

Ōmori, S., et al. (2020). *Introduction to Zen training: A physical approach to meditation and mind-body training*. Tuttle Publishing, an imprint of Periplus Editions (HK) Ltd.

Park, J. Y. (2010). *Makers of modern Korean Buddhism*. State University of New York Press.

Sangharakshita. (1996). *Great Buddhists of the twentieth century*. Windhorse Publications.

Sasaki, R. F., & Kirchner, T. Y. (2009). *The record of Linji*. Univ. of Hawai'i Press.

Seager, R. H. (2012). *Buddhism in America*. Columbia University Press.

Sharf, R. (1995a). Buddhist modernism and the rhetoric of meditative experience. *Numen, 42*(3), 228–283. https://doi.org/10.1163/1568527952598549

Sharf, R. H. (1995b). Sanbōkyōdan: Zen and the way of the new religions. *Japanese Journal of Religious Studies, 22*(3–4). https://doi.org/10.18874/jjrs.22.3-4.1995.417-458

Shore, J. (1996). *Koan Zen from the inside*. Retrieved May 8, 2023, from https://beingwithoutself.files.wordpress.com/2011/10/koan-zen-from-the-inside.pdf

Shute, J. (2018). Why 'Tibetan Buddhism is facing up to its own abuse scandal'. *The Telegraph*. Retrieved May 11, 2023, from https://www.telegraph.co.uk/news/2018/09/09/tibetan-buddhism-facing-abuse-scandal/

Smoley, R. (2010). Against Blavatsky: Rene Guenon's critique of theosophy. *Quest, 98*(1), 28–34.

Stirling, I. (2006). *Zen Pioneer: The life & works of Ruth Fuller Sasaki*. Shoemaker & Hoard.

Suzuki, D. T. (1964). *An introduction to Zen Buddhism. With a Foreword by Dr. Carl G. Jung*. Grove Press.

Suzuki, S., & Dixon, T. (2020). *Zen Mind, beginner's mind*. Shambhala.

Watts, A. W. (1963). *Psychotherapy, East and West*. Pantheon.

Watts, A. W. (1973). *In my own way*. Random House Pantheon.

Wick, P., & Rabens, V. (2014). *Religions and trade religious formation, transformation, and cross-cultural exchange between East and West*. Brill.

5

Psychology Discovers Zen

One of the foundations of the various traditions of Buddhism is overcoming the sufferings and ailments naturally encountered in the course of life, by travelling the Middle Way. It will therefore not be surprising that at the end of the nineteenth century, thinkers began to consider how aspects of Buddhism could be used to treat forms of mental suffering. It was at this time that in Europe, psychiatry was developing as a medical discipline concerned with the classification, diagnosis and treatment of mental disorders. Japanese physicians also began to be interested in Western psychiatry and were faced with the difficulties of framing the essentially Western edifice of psychiatry in Japanese culture and reality, as analysed by Karen Nakamura in her *A Disability of the Soul* (Nakamura, 2013).

Before considering how various approaches including Buddhist principles were introduced into psychiatric and psychological care in the West, it is worth exploring how some ideas relevant to this field emerged independently in Asia. In Japan at the beginning of the twentieth century, Shoma Morita, a contemporary of Sigmund Freud, founded what was called *Morita therapy*, a strictly structured approach that was influenced by some aspects of Zen Buddhism, and which aimed to treat a

T. Giraldi, *Zen Buddhism and the Reality of Suffering*,
https://doi.org/10.1007/978-3-031-69244-4_5

number of anxiety disorders, defined in Japan as *shinkeishitsu* (Morita & Morita, 1998). Morita's work was accompanied in the 1940s by Yoshimoto Ishin's *Naikan therapy*, a structured self-reflection that was proposed for use in psychotherapy (Krech, 2022a, 2022b; Reynolds, 1989).

Both approaches were initiated in Japan, and Morita therapy in particular began to be considered in both Europe and America, where it gained a certain acceptance. The efficacy of *Morita therapy* for treating anxiety disorders in adults has since been tested using evidence-based medical trials (Wu et al., 2015). *Naikan therapy* has also been explored in some detail in the context of intercultural ethnographic exchange (Silva, 2007).

It has to be noted, however, that Morita and Naikan therapies were developed in the unique anthropological context of Japan, based on specific societal and cultural perspectives on the individual perception of suffering and mental disorders. The foundations of psychiatry and psychology, which were made in Europe, had to be subsequently adopted in Japan with all the difficulties of integrating concepts from one profoundly different culture to another, differences to do with not only the classification of diagnostic entities but also their representation and perception. These complexities became a real practical challenge when pharmaceutical companies tried to introduce to Japan the same psychotropic drugs which had been used in biological psychiatry after the Second World War. This became even clearer during the ensuing epidemic of depression diagnoses in the USA and the resulting boom in the prescription of antidepressant drugs (Giraldi, 2017).

In addition to the *shinkeishitsu*, the anxiety-based disorders treated with Morita therapy, other new concepts appeared, such as *kokoro na kaze*, the 'cold of the soul' used to describe mild depression. There was also *utsubyo* for 'incurable depression', and *jase,* referring to problems in the mother-child dynamic, sometimes referred to as the 'Oedipus complex' in the West. In Japan, this was addressed with *Naikan therapy* (Watters & Healy, 2011; Silva, 2007).

Naikan, meaning introspection, was the term chosen to describe the structured method of self-reflection developed by Yoshimoto Ishin, a devout Jodo Shinshu Buddhist, in the 1940s. The practice is usually based on week-long retreats, when participants keep asking themselves three questions about a person's life: What did I receive from this person; What did I return to this person; and What troubles, worries, unhappiness did I cause this person? It established itself in Japan and later put down roots in Europe, particularly in Austria and Germany (Krech, 2022a, 2022b; Silva, 2009).

These approaches sit within a theoretical and procedural framework for intervention which bears the deep marks of its Japanese origin. Morita therapy is significantly influenced by Zen Buddhism, likely because of its founder's Zen training. Naikan therapy on the other hand does not appear to display any evident relationship to Zen, which is quite surprising since the notion of *naikan* was referred to extensively by Hakuin Ekaku, a figure who lived at the end of the seventeenth and beginning of the eighteenth century, and who was a key reformer who helped define Zen as we understand it today. Hakuin expounds *naikan* in a document entitled *Orategama*, where he emphasises that 'the true practice of introspection is an absolute essential that must never be neglected'. For Hakuin, the true practice of introspection (*naikan*) consists of a series of contemplations similar to deep meditation, focusing 'in the area below my navel down to my loins and the soles of my feet'.

Naikan, however, is a term with a variety of meanings. Hakuin appears to use it strictly in terms of contemplation or introspection that has therapeutic benefits, and insists on the extension of the practice of meditation into all the activities of daily life. *Orategama* is, in effect, an extremely rich and detailed guide to meditation. Hakuin strongly insists on the need for concentration acquired through a deep state of meditation on the *tanden*, an area specifically located in the abdomen below the navel, and extending to the lower part of the body, particularly involving the soles of the feet. For Hakuin, this practice must be embedded into the aspects of daily life.

Orategama was written by Hakuin in response to a letter received from the Governor of the Province of Settsu. It is outstanding in clarifying all the crucial aspects of a clear and pure practice of Zen. One aspect which is quite unique is that Hakuin refers to the contemplations he proposes as an addition to the practice of meditation and koans, as something that can provide evident therapeutic benefits, especially while ageing (Yampolsky, 1971):

This statement might seem to contrast with the general view that the only aim of the practice is the practice itself, and the realisation of awakening. However, it might not conflict with the evidence that by following Hakuin's advice for pure practice, positive bodily outcomes are also attained.

One pioneering practitioner who attempted to overcome the difficulty of bringing together the diametrically opposed Japanese and Western cultures, and their perspectives on using Zen meditation as a psychotherapeutic intervention, was Tomio Hirai. Born in 1927, Tomio Hirai graduated from the Medical School of the University of Tokyo in 1950 and had an outstanding career, becoming a professor in the University Hospital Faculty of Medicine's Department of Psychiatry in Tokyo. He later became president of the Japanese Society of Psychiatry and Neurology and director of the Japan Mental Health Association until his death in 1993 (Tomio Hiray (1927–1993), n.d.).

During his professional life, he became a recognised authority on the study of Zen meditation, zazen, and its use as a treatment for neurotic disorders, including the bodily changes that occur during meditation. He was convinced that Zen meditation was effective as a psychotherapeutic intervention, and his investigations on the psychophysiology of zazen are of even greater interest. Indeed, they were the first attempt to employ the best techniques available after the end of the Second World War for studying the central and peripheral nervous system's response to various psychological conditions. These investigations show an accurate understanding of the basic theoretical and practical aspects of traditional Zen and zazen. This was a consequence of the fact that the examination of Zen meditators was performed in a main Soto Zen monastery in Kyoto, Eiheiji, where no lay visitor or investigator had ever been granted permission to perform scientific studies on the monks. As a Japanese university professor, and thanks to letters of introduction, Hirai could perform his studies in the temple with all the necessary experimental tools and instruments.

It is worth noting that the monks examined had been at the temple for a long time, and in the analysis of the results, they were ranked on the basis of years of experience: 0 to 5, 5 to 20, and 20 to 40. This is comparable to the timescale necessary for the full training of monks as masters and before being granted the formal title of roshi.

The techniques used were mainly electroencephalography (EEG), as well as the recording of electromyograms, respiratory functions and galvanic skin responses. The results obtained were also published in English and subsequently translated into other languages, soon gaining significant attention. The results of the EEG studies were initially published in a scientific journal (Kasamatsu & Hirai, 1966), and wider reports covering the studies in detail were subsequently published in three books entitled *Zen Meditation Therapy* (Hirai, 1975), *Zen and the Mind. Scientific Approach to Zen Practice* (Hirai, 1978), and *Zen Meditation and Psychotherapy* (Hirai, 1989). In essence, Hirai argued that Zen meditation can be a useful therapeutic tool for the treatment of neurotic mental conditions. During zazen, specific bodily changes were observed, with the EEG showing distinctive brain waves that led Hirai to argue that a specific mental state of consciousness was occurring, different from that observed after transcendental meditation, hypnosis, yoga, autogenic training and Morita therapy.

These studies of zazen psychophysiology and therapeutic potential have the benefit of being accessible to both Japanese and Western audiences. They were conducted in a Zen temple, with Zen monks, in conditions which have changed irreversibly in the following decades, and are now essentially non-replicable. They were also anticipatory and have inspired many who later studied the therapeutic potential and the physiological mechanisms accompanying Buddhist meditation.

At the same time, and independently from this interest in Zen and psychotherapy in Japan, Buddhism was attracting the attention of eminent Western figures, and it is probably significant that many of these early interests regarded psychoanalysts. Carl Gustav Jung is one, who during his long and productive life produced profound and original contributions on the understanding of the human psyche; his works include also deep and original considerations about religions, with particular attention to Buddhism and Zen (McLynn, 1998). One well-known contribution is the foreword to D.T. Suzuki's *Introduction to Zen Buddhism*, which, after its first appearance in German before the Second World War, was later translated into English after the end of the war (Suzuki, 1964).

Jung himself was not a Buddhist, apparently did not formally practice any of the Buddhist traditions, and had a solely intellectual interest in the subject. He wrote on the psychology of Western meditation, on the *Tibetan Book of the Great Liberation* and on the *Tibetan Book of the Dead*, in addition to his contributions to Zen. He displayed a remarkably deep understanding of Buddhism, gained through intellectual introspection, while his works show an admirable understanding of Buddhism's core values and deserve substantial consideration. The authoritative work on this is Meckel and Moore's *Self and Liberation—The Jung-Buddhism Dialogue* (Meckel et al., 1992).

It is clearly impossible to try to render in a few lines the rich and complex thoughts of Jung on Buddhism. One statement in particular, however, is worth considering in some depth because of its lapidary concision: 'The goal in psychotherapy is exactly the same as in Buddhism'.

It was made during a conversation between Jung and Hisamatsu, which is reported in the book edited by Young-Eisendrath and Muramoto, *Awakening and Insight. Zen Buddhism and Psychotherapy* (Young-Eisendrath & Muramoto, 2003a).

A similarly brief and relevant statement is made by Masao Abe in his chapter entitled *The Self in Jung and Zen* in the book edited by Meckel and Moore:

> The most conspicuous difference between Buddhism and western psychology is perhaps found in their respective treatments of the concept of 'self.' In western psychology, the existence of a 'self' is generally affirmed; Buddhism denies the existence of an enduring 'self' and substitutes instead the concept of *anatman*, 'no-self.' [Meckel et al., 1992]

It is worth noting that Jung had a rich series of exchanges with Shinichi Hisamatsu, a Japanese thinker who interspersed his studies of philosophy with explorations of Rinzai Zen, which he practised under the master Ikegami Shosan during his monastic life at Myoshinji, before becoming a professor at the University of Kyoto. Hisamatsu is little known outside restricted circles, especially in the West, but he is highly esteemed by many Zen masters and scholars in Japan (Meckel et al., 1992). Masao Abe, who was cited above, entered Kyoto University as a philosopher, where he deepened and perfected his studies and his practice of Zen under the guidance of Hisamatsu, providing valuable contributions to the Western understanding of Zen. After the death of Daisetz Teitaro Suzuki, he became one of the main representatives of Zen Buddhism in Europe and North America (Abe & LaFleur, 1989).

Jung's interest in Buddhism and Zen was a precursor to other psychoanalysts engaging with the subject, as many have continued to do until the present day. An early contribution which became a classic for all those interested either in psychology or Zen Buddhism is *Zen Buddhism and Psychoanalysis*, which contains *Lectures on Zen Buddhism* by Daisetz Teitaro Suzuki, *Psychoanalysis and Zen Buddhism* by Erich Fromm, and *The Human Situation and Zen Buddhism* by Richard De Martino. These contributions were originally presented during a workshop on *Zen Buddhism and Psychoanalysis* held in Cuernavaca, Mexico, in August 1957 at the Department of Psychoanalysis of the Medical School of the Autonomous National University of Mexico (Fromm et al., 1970). Mexico seems to have been a live crucible for experiences like this in the 1960s. Ejo Takata, a monk who completed his Zen training under Yamada Mumon Roshi at Myoshinji in Kyoto, established himself in Mexico City where he lived until his death. He was involved in various activities, including social engagement and supporting peasants, in addition to his role as a Zen master. One of his pupils was Alejandro Jodorowsky, who later became director of various cult movies and also developed a unique psychotherapy that he called '*psicomagia*' (Jodorowsky et al., 2016; Jodorowsky, 2004).

Several figures in psychoanalysis later independently discovered Zen and undertook their training in America progressed along the Way pointed out by Japanese masters and their successors. In many cases, they also started and ran Zen centres and temples in different parts of the country and published their contributions about Zen Buddhism and psychoanalysis. Barry Magid is one, who focused on Self Psychology, based on the school founded by Heinz Kohut. While he was training, he started his Zen practice first under Eido Tai Shimano, and afterwards under Charlotte Joko Beck, the Dharma heir of Taizan Maezumi. He later established *The Ordinary Mind Zendo* in New York City, where he teaches a psychologically focused form of Soto Zen and *shikantaza*. He also initiated his own lineage with his American disciples (Ford, 2006). Magid has written a number of books about the integration of psychoanalysis and Zen: *Ordinary Mind: Exploring the Common Ground of Zen and Psychoanalysis* (Magid, 2002), *Ending the Pursuit of Happiness* (Magid, 2008) and *Nothing Is Hidden: The Psychology of Zen Koan* (Magid, 2013).

Mark Epstein has also explored the mind both through psychiatry and Buddhism. In his early 20s, after his encounter with Buddhism through his first American teachers Goldstein and Kornfeld, he travelled to Ajan Chah's forest monastery in Thailand, where he learned the practice of insight meditation. He trained as a psychiatrist at Harvard Medical School and started his private practice of psychiatry in New York City, also holding a position in New York University School of Medicine (Epstein, 2020). His is focused especially on traumatic experiences, together with the relevance of the self in psychotherapy. He has authored several books, including *Psychotherapy Without the Self: A Buddhist Perspective* (Epstein, 2008), *Thoughts Without a Thinker: Psychotherapy from a Buddhist Perspective* (Epstein, 2013) and *The Zen of Therapy: Uncovering a Hidden Kindness in Life* (Epstein, 2023).

The books mentioned so far are by authors whose thought is psychoanalytically oriented, discovering Buddhism as a practice they happened to embrace after training as psychoanalysts. These are, however, just a part of the contributions on Buddhist meditation, Zen and psychotherapy.

One early essay is *Psychotherapy East and West* by Alan W. Watts, one of the key figures in the West's early encounters with Buddhism, who wrote several books destined to become bestsellers on the subject (Watts, 1963).

In the following years, repeated efforts were made to collect the qualified experiences which became available as more work was done in psychology and psychotherapy to explore the common ground between Eastern and Western thought. John Welwood edited a remarkable variety of experiences in *Awakening the Heart. East/West Approaches to Psychotherapy and the Healing Relationship*. These were from experts with a wide variety of different backgrounds and included, to name just a few, Jack Kornfeld, Mokusan Miyuki, Erich Fromm, Joshu Sasaki Roshi, Chogyam Trungpa and David Brandon (Welwood, 1983). Brandon in particular had a unique experience, since his involvement was mainly focused on social issues. He was a social worker engaged in assisting disadvantaged communities, which he pursued as an intense realisation of his Buddhist and Zen faith outside the world of theory and doctrine (Brandon, 2017). Guy Claxton edited a similar collection, based on varied contributions, entitled *Beyond Therapy. The Impact of Eastern Religions on Psychological Theory and Practice* (Claxton, 1996).

David Brazier has provided interesting and rich contributions on these subjects. He joined his own experience of meditation and Buddhism as a spiritual teacher of the Order of Amida Buddha, with his activity as a registered psychotherapist and holder of a doctorate in Buddhist psychology. As the leader of the Amida Order, he focused this religious community on socially engaged Buddhism on the international stage, particularly on projects in Africa, Asia and Eastern Europe. In early 2020, in response to the COVID pandemic, he helped found the Global Sangha, an international virtual network centred on the Buddhist teachings of Buddha Amitabha, Nembutsu Pure Land Way (The weblog of David Brazier; David Brazier at La Ville au Roi).

Brazier does not appear to have had formal Zen training, yet he published a book entitled *Zen Therapy*, which provides a deep, clear and direct description of the aspects of Buddhism that are relevant to psychology and psychotherapy. Part three of the book, entitled *Therapy as a Zen Way*, delves in particular into the core aspects of psychotherapy, seen from a Buddhist perspective. Frazier's career and work span a long time, and he actively continues it with Eleusis, a collection of projects such as the Global Sangha, the International Zen Therapy Institute and La Ville au Roi Hermitage, of which he is director (David Brazier at La Ville au Roi (Eleusis), 2023). Brazier is also a clear example of the humanistic view that can arise when Buddhist values are integrated with the person-centred psychotherapies inspired by personalities such as Carl Rogers (Brazier, 1998).

Work has also been done to explore the religious implications of this intersection, for example, in terms of the Hinayana South East Asian traditions (Kwee, 2015), as well as the relationships between psychotherapy and religion in Japan (Silva, 2009). The psychoanalytic aspects have been studied through Jungian analytic psychology (Kawai, 2008), as well as the more general integration of psychology, psychoanalysis and

Buddhism (Rubin, 2013). Particularly rich and detailed analysis on this especially in relation to Zen can be found in *Awakening and Insight; Zen Buddhism and Psychotherapy*, edited by Young-Eisendrath and Muramoto (Young-Eisendrath & Muramoto, 2003a, 2003b). Additional contributions on the integration of a Buddhist approach into the clinical setting, including the technical aspects of this, can be found in *Self and No-Self*, which considers Eastern and Western perspectives on analytical psychology, psychoanalysis and Buddhism (Mathers et al., 2009). There are more contributions on this subject in Welwood's *Toward a Psychology of Awakening: Buddhism, Psychotherapy, and the Path of Personal and Spiritual Transformation* (Welwood, 2002).

Buddhism, psychoanalysis and psychology appear to have some common grounds in terms of their view of the mind, its expression during an individual's life trajectory and the existential sufferings, delusions and illusions which accompany it. The various traditions and schools of Buddhism that developed from the initial teachings of the historical Buddha 2500 years ago share a doctrinal core which reveals a clear and deep phenomenological understanding and description of the human mind. Meanwhile, the Western understanding of the human mind and its disorders and existential sufferings began between the nineteenth and twentieth centuries thanks to two crucial events: the founding of psychoanalysis and the beginning of psychology as a new experimental science of the mind, based on the natural sciences and physiology.

Psychoanalysis merits particular consideration for several reasons. Its founder, Sigmund Freud, was a highly prolific writer for a period which spans from his first contributions at the end of the nineteenth century until his death in 1939. His numerous works were remarkable first contributions in many areas and are still of great relevance today. Concepts such as the Id, Ego and Super-ego, the unconscious, the Oedipus complex and libido, the analysis of dreams, the defence mechanisms and resistance, and neurotic complexes, together with the method of free association in analysis, have become culturally ubiquitous beyond academia and professional practice.

Psychoanalysis was initially received with a mixture of attraction and resistance; after some initial enthusiasm, it declined decisively as a clinical practice. Yet psychoanalytic concepts continue to retain their cultural relevance, and some of these principles are still pervasive in psychology, psychotherapy and psychiatry and retain a substantial presence in the wider humanities. Freud can also be seen as the progenitor of the 'talking cure'.

The history of psychoanalysis is very rich, and just a few points may be recalled here. It is particularly worth noting that a structured association was organised among Freud's followers to protect the principles of psychoanalysis. With time, this provided the basis for doctrinal orthodoxy and hierarchy. An effect of this was the publication of an approved biography of Freud by Ernest Jones, which became a classic reference point (Jones, 1974). Another masterly and enthusiastic biography was written by the celebrated Austrian writer Stefan Zweig, *Mental healers*, which also traced the lives of Franz Anton Mesmer and Mary Baker Eddy (Zweig, 1969). Many aspects of these biographies are hagiographic, and new access to Freud's papers has recently shed greater light on his life and thought (Borch-Jacobsen & Shamdasani, 2012). Another recent, balanced biographical contribution was written by Peter Gay (Gay, 1988).

The development of psychoanalysis induced contrasting views, varying from an enthusiastic acceptance to strong resistance and rejection. Indeed, more serious and articulated criticisms have been made of the entire structure of psychoanalysis. One of the best known is from the prominent philosopher Karl Popper, who argued that psychoanalysis is a pseudoscience because its claims are not testable, cannot be refuted, and cannot be subjected to the test of falsifiability. In one of his writings, Popper goes as far as stating:

> ...those 'clinical observations' which analysts naively believe confirm their theory cannot do this any more than the daily confirmations which astrologers find in their practice. And as for Freud's epic of the Ego, the Superego, and the Id, no substantially stronger claim to scientific status can be made for it than for Homer's collected stories from the Olympus. (Popper, 1992)

Other critics include Michel Onfray, who has carefully detailed a number of philosophical contradictions he identifies in Freud's writings (Onfray, 2011). Jeffrey Moussaief Masson is a prolific scholar, a Freudian analyst, and an author who took a severely critical position expressed in his book *Against Therapy: Emotional Tyranny and the Myth of Psychological Healing*. His criticisms are addressed to not only approaches directly based on Freud's writing and theories but also other approaches inspired by Freudian principles, such as humanistic psychology, as well as family and gestalt therapy (Masson, 1988).

One central point in the critiques of psychoanalysis is the refutation of the idea that it is a psychotherapy. The effects of the analytic process on the individual being analysed are not evaluated using the same objective criteria used for other medical and psychiatric interventions. Analysis proposes itself to be a process involving the whole person which should not be reduced to the frame of a sanitary treatment.

At the same time, it is evident that a number of the psychotherapies which originated with psychoanalysis have retained some of its principles, which are likely present in any effective therapeutic alliance between the therapist and their patient. One first principle is that neurosis and neurotic sufferings originate from an imaginary or real psychological trauma, whose consequences become unconscious and inaccessible to deliberate awareness while affecting the individual's emotions and behaviours. Neurotic mental sufferings are therefore considered a functional, or rather dysfunctional, reactive mental condition, caused by difficulties of adaptation to existential life events. They thus are of reactive and functional origin, are therefore reversible, and can be attenuated through the use of the 'talking cure' in a way that would be termed *psychodynamic*.

Moreover, phenomena of transference and countertransference occur during the process of analysis and psychotherapy, and the therapist has to be capable of successfully identifying and using them in the therapeutic process.

Finally, psychoanalysts have to undergo specific training, which is based on the study of the theoretical basis of the analytic process. Even more relevant is the requirement to undergo personal analysis with an authorised trainer. After having successfully completed this, the analysts are still in training and are allowed to begin their activity and develop their professional experience only under strict supervision. Only at the end of this path can they be accepted into their professional association as certified analysts.

These basic principles were followed at the beginning of Freudian psychoanalysis, when first Freud then his loyal early disciples, trained others. This led to the foundation of national and international psychoanalytic associations, which adhered to Freud's works and basic principles in an attempt to guarantee doctrinal homogeneity. Early on, there were also a number of figures who proposed a variety of approaches and techniques. Prominent analysts such as Carl Gustav Jung and Alferd Adler are examples of those initiated by Freud who soon detached from the Freudian orthodoxy; other significant and more recent figures are neo-Freudians such as Erich Fromm, Jaques Lacan and their followers (Brennan & Houde, 2023).

Psychoanalysis was the inspiration for the development of a variety of psychotherapies which shared some of its basic values. Life's existential ailments could be seen through the open, humanistic, person-centred and psychodynamic perspective of reactive and reversible principles. And it is evident how, when the core messages of Buddhism were considered, they could enrich the therapeutic approaches of a number of Western psychotherapists.

It is worth noting that the training of psychoanalysts and psychotherapists inspires some comparison with the training of Buddhist monks and masters. In both cases, the beginners have a teacher, whose authority must be uncritically accepted. The trainee then follows their teacher's guidance in a process of individual personal analysis and therapy, or of religious practice in a training monastery, for a previously unspecified duration. At the end of the process, the trainee can secure the highly sought final qualification and be admitted to the lineage of their training analyst or Buddhist master, and may begin their work as a qualified therapist or teacher. It is quite apparent that this, at least in theory, guarantees that the therapist (or master) has a direct experience of the process through which they lead their trainee (or disciple), and which adds to the certification of their competence.

A completely different series of events occurred with 'talking cures', with the first development of behaviourism. This approach would grow and change dramatically, and some of its principles came to be included in the foundations of the new 'cognitive behavioural therapy' (CBT), and its later second and third waves of development, which would become highly popular. The foundations of CBT are profoundly different from those of other existing psychodynamic approaches.

CBT is an intervention which was developed by Aaron Beck to reduce the symptoms of mental health conditions such as depression and anxiety. It is a 'problem-focused' and 'action-oriented' form of therapy used to treat specific problems diagnosed as a mental disorder. This is proposed to be achieved by changing thoughts, beliefs and attitudes and their associated behaviours, in order to improve cognitive distortions and emotional regulation (Beck, 2021).

The distance from psychodynamic approaches could not be greater. First, a diagnosis of a mental condition has to be made; second, the effects of the treatment have to be evaluated by adopting a measure of the outcome. Some problems immediately appear, relating to the diagnosis and outcome. CBT largely relies on the diagnostic criteria of the American Psychiatric Association's *Diagnostic and Statistical Manual of Mental Disorders* (DSM) whose first edition was published in 1952, followed by several editions including the fifth, which appeared in 2013 and was published as *DSM-5-TR* in 2020.

The DSM immediately attracted serious criticism, since every distance from a norm defined by a diagnostic criterion led to the formal diagnosis of a mental disorder. Additionally, psychometric scales prepared for the purpose could be used for diagnosis and also for the evaluation of the severity of the condition before and after the treatment. Unlike psychoanalysis, CBT subjected its efficacy to tests based on the criteria of inclusion and outcome and used the 'gold standard' more commonly used in the trials of psychotropic drugs (Giraldi, 2017). It is not surprising that after psychoanalysis, CBT and its variations also attracted their own critiques (Beidel & Turner, 1986; Burkeman, 2016). A large literature thus appeared, and substantial debates about psychodynamic and cognitive behavioural therapies persist to the present.

One curious point to note here is that presumably in order to distance themselves from the traditional, post-Freudian 'talking cures', the proponents of cognitive behavioural psychotherapies have defined their practice as a 'therapy' rather than a 'psychotherapy', perhaps to imply their proximity to sciences.

Remarkably, cognitive and behavioural approaches also discovered Buddhism and imagined a new common ground between Western and Eastern approaches to the human mind and its ailments. This initially happened when the new 'mindfulness' movement was proposed in the late 1990s in the United States by Jon Kabat-Zinn. The essence of it was the use of Buddhist meditation deprived of Buddhism, to fight stress and depression in a new medically verified approach. With time, mindfulness progressively lost almost all of its connection with Buddhist meditation, while acquiring extreme and pervasive popularity. 'Mindfulness', the *sati* of the Eightfold Buddhist Path in the Buddhist scriptures, thus gained a new life, at the same time becoming progressively and substantially detached from Buddhism; its instructors and therapists have no significant knowledge and experience of Buddhism and Buddhist meditation.

From its original use for fighting stress, mindfulness was extended to attempt to ease many other mental afflictions, and the world of cognitivism and cognitive-based therapies, such as CBT, became interested in mindfulness, in spite of the distance between CBT and its distance from Buddhist meditation; new approaches were developed, such as Mindfulness-Based Cognitive Therapy. In fact, the role of meditation came to be progressively reduced until it largely disappeared from the structure of the cognitively based approach. The name of mindfulness was retained, but the initial promise to connect it with Buddhist meditation practices was de facto abandoned (Giraldi, 2020). Some of these points deserve more attention and will be examined in greater detail in the following chapters; the remainder of the present one will consider some of the intersections between psychotherapies and Zen Buddhism.

Indeed, since the early work of Sigmund Freud, numerous psychotherapies have been developed by practitioners who criticised the original Freudian approach on theoretical grounds. A host of innovators and innovations followed and have continued to appear since; Scott O. Lilienfeld and Hal Arkowitz in a 2012 article estimated the existence of at least 500 different types of psychotherapy. The most widespread approaches were grouped as behaviour therapies (altering unhealthy behaviours), cognitive-behaviour therapies (altering maladaptive ways of thinking), psychodynamic therapy (resolving unconscious conflicts and adverse childhood experiences), interpersonal therapy (remedying unhealthy ways of interacting with others) and person-centred therapy (helping clients to find their own solutions to life's problems; Lilienfeld & Arkowitz, 2012).

The development of more and more new approaches, as well as refinements and variations on previous ones, raises the question of whether the new proposals are justified, theoretically and in terms of clinical efficacy. The question is reasonable and obvious: Rosenzweig expressed it in an article entitled *Some Implicit Common Factors in Diverse Methods of Psychotherapy* published as far as 1936. The subtitle, *At Last the Dodo said, 'Everybody Has Won, and All Must Have Prizes'* is from Lewis Carroll's 1865 book, *Alice in Wonderland*, where the Dodo bird decided to issue a competition to run around the lake for a number of wet characters in order to dry themselves, and nobody cared to get a finishing order. Rosenzweig argued that whether or not common factors were responsible for the outcomes of different psychotherapies, as with the Dodo's judgement, all therapies are winners, and all produce equally effective outcomes (Rosenzweig, 1936).

This subject rose again substantially in the 1970s when the debate about the effectiveness of various psychotherapies attracted significant attention and sparked a number of original investigations, reports, reviews and critical reviews of the literature and meta-analyses. Meta-analysis in particular became a more and more common tool for investigating numerous small studies which were amassing, and by using new methods of statistical analysis, it enabled researchers to draw conclusions which would otherwise have been impossible.

In 1997, Wampold and his collaborators tested the Dodo bird conjecture, examining a vast sample of the available literature, and found that the magnitude of the effects from different treatments was similar, with minor differences. Their conclusion was that the evidence supported the conjecture that the efficacy of bona fide treatments is roughly equivalent (Wampold et al., 1997).

In more general terms, it is not surprising that there are many investigations still being carried out, with a similarly large variety of techniques and subjects, into the efficacy of psychotherapies, reporting a similarly wide variety of results. A recent study examined a large number of articles published on the subject, aiming to answer the question 'does psychotherapy work'. The authors cautiously comment that the large-scale umbrella review identified prominent biases in the psychotherapy field, as almost half of the meta-analyses showed large heterogeneity, evidence provided by small study, or a combination of the above. Of the 247 studies considered, only 7 per cent provided convincing evidence that psychotherapy is effective: these pertained to cognitive behavioural therapy, cognitive remediation, counselling, mixed types of psychotherapies and meditation therapy, which had the most robust evidence (together with CBT) for anxiety symptoms (Dragioti et al., 2017).

Aaron Beck's development of CBT in the 1960s and 1970s had a great impact on the archipelago of 'talking cures', rapidly establishing itself as a treatment for several mental disorders in the fields of the cognitive sciences and psychiatry. CBT rapidly replaced psychoanalytically oriented interventions in medicine, and it deeply influenced psychiatry, in North America in particular. This happened thanks to significant effort to demonstrate its efficacy in a large number of clinical trials performed following the principles of evidence-based medicine. The question whether CBT is really more effective than the psychodynamic interventions it replaced still remains debated.

In 2011, Shedler used a rigorous methodology to examine the evidence in the published studies, concluding:

> Empirical evidence supports the efficacy of psychodynamic therapy. Effect sizes for psychodynamic therapy are as large as those reported for other therapies that have been actively promoted as 'empirically supported' and 'evidence based.' In addition, patients who receive psychodynamic therapy maintain therapeutic gains and appear to continue to improve after treatment ends. Finally, non-psychodynamic therapies may be effective in part because the more skilled practitioners utilize techniques that have long been central to psychodynamic theory and practice. The perception that psychodynamic approaches lack empirical support does not accord with available scientific evidence and may reflect selective dissemination of research findings.

The effects of psychodynamic therapies were as great, or even greater than those of CBT; the only evident difference was the inferiority of antidepressant medication (Shedler, 2011).

The efficacy for psychodynamic therapy in comparison with other empirically supported treatments such as CBT is still a crucial issue that draws substantial interest. The results obtained by Steinert and her collaborators have shown yet again the equivalence of psychodynamic therapy with other treatments, and the study also explores who might benefit most from which treatment (Steinert et al., 2017).

The initial positive results published for CBT seem, in essence, to have been scaled down in subsequent years (Johnsen & Friborg, 2015). The recent evidence gathered with rigorous accuracy confirms the remarkable efficacy of psychoanalytic psychotherapy, raising the question of the need for an evaluation including a long-term follow-up where psychodynamic interventions may show their superiority (Fonagy et al., 2015).

The studies which have been considered so far have been made using rigorous methods chosen by the study authors, in terms of the selection of the experimental conditions and subjects for the investigations, the diagnosis of the condition treated, the nature of the intervention examined, the criteria for evaluating the outcome, and the procedures for statistical analysis. The best procedure which was devised after the Second World War for the evaluation of medical treatments is evidence-based medicine conducted by using randomised clinical trials (RCT) including also a placebo. This became the accepted gold standard for medical somatic studies and produced accurate, objective results when the efficacy (and safety) of clinical interventions was evaluated.

When these procedures were used for research in psychiatry and psychotherapy, however, new challenges arose that led to unsatisfactory results. Indeed, one of the crucial parts of the design of an RCT is the use of a placebo intervention. The subjects of the study are randomly split into groups, one receiving the full treatment under evaluation, and the other receiving the same treatment but without its active ingredient, which is replaced by an inactive one, the placebo. The subjects, the staff who deliver the treatment, and those who judge its effects have to ignore who receives the real intervention and who receives the sham one, the so-called 'double blind' procedure. This makes it possible to subtract the magnitude of the effects observed in the placebo group from those observed in the group receiving the treatment including the active ingredient, thus showing its specific effectiveness. The challenge of creating a placebo group for a defined psychotherapeutic intervention, compared to a real one, is evident. The result is that RCTs, the best objective procedure available, could only be used for comparing the magnitude of the effects of two different *active* interventions but not for comparing any efficacy against an inert placebo. These difficulties are well known, as clearly reported in a recent article by Fava and his large group of collaborators (Guidi et al., 2018).

These problems have also been addressed by Bruce E. Wampold, a researcher who has provided valuable contributions in this area. His article, *Where Oh Where Are the Specific Ingredients?*, directly addresses this issue (Ahn & Wampold, 2001), and he covers this challenge in greater detail in his book, *The Psychotherapy Debate* (Wampold & Imel, 2015). Wampold shows that only about one per cent of the overall therapeutic effectiveness of psychotherapy is ascribable to the specific intervention, and about 7 per cent is due to the strength of the therapeutic alliance established between therapist and client. The remaining 90 per cent, Wampold demonstrates, is caused by other factors which have been poorly explored, such as the personalities of the therapist and client.

Wampold later identified among these a constellation of common factors including alliance, empathy, expectations, cultural adaptation and therapist differences, all of which are involved in the effectiveness of psychotherapies. He thus outlined a *contextual model*, based on four factors which are related to the benefits of psychotherapy: treatment differences, specific ingredients, adherence, and competence (Wampold, 2015).

The competence of the therapist and the capacity to establish a positive therapeutic alliance with the client were evidenced as crucial issues also when in 1974 D.F. Ricks described the results obtained by two therapists working at a major child guidance centre. The long-term outcomes of the two therapists were not different for less disturbed clients. However, striking differences emerged in their therapeutic styles and outcomes when working with the more emotionally disturbed boys. Comparing the two therapists, 27 per cent treated by one, in comparison to 85 per cent treated by the other, went on to develop adult schizophrenia. The more successful therapist was labelled *supershrink* by one of the boys, and Ricks retains this term to describe his techniques compared to those of the other therapist whom he called *pseudoshrink* (Ricks, 1974). Similar findings have been reported by Bergin and Suinn for another *pseudoshrink*: the boys treated by this therapist had adult adjustment that was alarmingly poor, in contrast to those treated by more effective *supershrink* (Bergin & Suinn, 1975). In the decades after these reports, there has been little research on the effects of the individual therapist (Lambert & Okiishi, 1997), as researchers have increasingly turned their attention away from effective therapy providers and to the search for effective psychotherapies (Chambless, 1995).

The issues considered so far indicate the existence of some common ground between Buddhism and psychology. One of the central messages of Buddhism is that mental ailments unavoidably accompany the trajectory of life, and that there is a path, the Middle Way, which points towards enlightenment, the freedom from the constraints of the ordinary mind, and hence the avoidance of the sufferings caused by attachment to the impermanent aspects of life. This might be one of the reasons why psychoanalysts were immediately attracted to Buddhism. Indeed, Freud used psychoanalysis to try to provide relief from neurotic suffering caused by specific psychological mechanisms, with his famous goal: 'to replace neurotic misery with ordinary unhappiness'.

The various Buddhist Schools that spread the basic teachings of Siddhartha Gautama in the East all share the same core message. The sufferings of existence are caused by the attachment of the individual self to impermanent aspects of life, and the realisation of the illusory nature of the self leads to enlightenment that makes it possible to see clearly the reality of the internal and external world, and enables liberation from life's existential sufferings.

Contemporary approaches to psychotherapy have adopted a similar aim, that is, to overcome the mental ailments which may accompany the course of an individual's life. Their precise aim, however, is more difficult to define because of the wide variety of psychotherapies. A key issue that may be perceived is the apparent analogy of Buddhist awakening in relation to the psychologists' *insight*, a state of awareness previously inaccessible, which allows an individual to overcome the difficulties of coping with the mental problems and ailments encountered when coping with life events. Some aspects of this have already been examined above. The question is so deep and varied, however, that it deserves greater exploration, from the various points of view that have been used to address it; this is the aim of the following chapters.

References

Abe, M., & LaFleur, W. R. (1989). *Zen and western thought*. University of Hawaii Press.

Ahn, H., & Wampold, B. E. (2001). Where oh where are the specific ingredients? A meta-analysis of component studies in counseling and psychotherapy. *Journal of Counseling Psychology, 48*(3), 251–257. https://doi.org/10.1037/0022-0167.48.3.251

Beck, J. S. (2021). *Cognitive behavior therapy: Basics and beyond*. The Guilford Press.

Beidel, D. C., & Turner, S. M. (1986). A critique of the theoretical bases of cognitive behavioral theories and therapy. *Clinical Psychology Review, 6*(2), 177–197. https://doi.org/10.1016/0272-7358(86)90011-5

Bergin, A. E., & Suinn, R. M. (1975). Individual psychotherapy and behavior therapy. *Annual Review of Psychology, 26*(1), 509–556. https://doi.org/10.1146/annurev.ps.26.020175.002453

Borch-Jacobsen, M., & Shamdasani, S. (2012). *The Freud files: An inquiry into the history of psychoanalysis*. Cambridge University Press.

Brandon, D. (2017). *Zen in the art of helping*. Taylor & Francis.

Brazier, D. (1998). *Beyond Carl Rogers: Towards a psychotherapy for the 21st Century*. Constable.

Brennan, J. F., & Houde, K. A. (2023). *History and systems of psychology*. Cambridge University Press.

Burkeman, O. (2016). Therapy wars: The revenge of Freud. *The Guardian*. Retrieved August 8, 2023, from https://www.theguardian.com/science/2016/jan/07/therapy-wars-revenge-of-freud-cognitive-behavioural-therapy

Chambless, D. L. (1995). Training in and dissemination of empirically-validated psychological treatments: Report and recommendations. *PsycEXTRA Dataset* [Preprint]. https://doi.org/10.1037/e554972011-003

Claxton, G. (1996). *Beyond therapy: The impact of eastern religions on psychological theory and practice*. Prism Press.

David Brazier at La Ville au roi (Eleusis). (2023). *David Brazier at La Ville au Roi (Eleusis)*. Retrieved July 25, 2023, from https://eleusis.ning.com/

Dragioti, E., et al. (2017). Does psychotherapy work? An umbrella review of meta-analyses of randomized controlled trials. *Acta Psychiatrica Scandinavica, 136*(3), 236–246. https://doi.org/10.1111/acps.12713

Epstein, M. (2008). *Psychotherapy without the self: A Buddhist perspective*. Yale University Press.

Epstein, M. (2013). *Thoughts without a thinker: Psychotherapy from a Buddhist perspective*. Basic Books.

Epstein, M. (2020). *Freud and Buddha, Network of Spiritual Progressives RSS*. Retrieved June 12, 2023, from https://web.archive.org/web/20140309194605/http://spiritualprogressives.org/newsite/?p=651

Epstein, M. (2023). *Zen of therapy: Uncovering a hidden kindness in life*. Penguin Books.

Fonagy, P., et al. (2015). Pragmatic randomized controlled trial of long-term psychoanalytic psychotherapy for treatment-resistant depression: The Tavistock Adult Depression Study (TADS). *World Psychiatry, 14*(3), 312–321. https://doi.org/10.1002/wps.20267

Ford, J. I. (2006). *Zen master who?: A guide to the people and stories of zen*. Wisdom Publications.

Fromm, E., Suzuki, D. T., & De Martino, R. (1970). *Zen Buddhism & psychoanalysis*. Harper and Row.

Gay, P. (1988). *Freud: A life for our times*. W.W. Norton.

Giraldi, T. (2017). *Unhappiness, sadness and 'depression': Antidepressants and the mental disorder epidemic*. Springer International Publishing.

Giraldi, T. (2020). *Psychotherapy, mindfulness and Buddhist meditation*. Palgrave Macmillan.

Guidi, J., et al. (2018). Methodological recommendations for trials of psychological interventions. *Psychotherapy and Psychosomatics, 87*(5), 276–284. https://doi.org/10.1159/000490574

Hirai, T. (1975). *Zen meditation therapy*. Japan Publications.

Hirai, T. (1978). *Zen and the mind: Scientific approach to Zen practice*. Japan Publications.

Hirai, T. (1989). *Zen meditation and psychotherapy*. Japan Publ.

Jodorowsky, A. (2004). *Psicomagia*. Siruela.

Jodorowsky, A., Bess, L., & Lhermillier, N. (2016). *Le Doigt et la lune: Histoires Zen*. Albin Michel.

Johnsen, T. J., & Friborg, O. (2015). The effects of cognitive behavioral therapy as an anti-depressive treatment is falling: A meta-analysis. *Psychological Bulletin, 141*(4), 747–768. https://doi.org/10.1037/bul0000015

Jones, E. (1974). *Sigmund Freud: Life and work*. Hogarth Press.

Kasamatsu, A., & Hirai, T. (1966). An electroencephalographic study on Zen meditation (zazen). *Psychiatry and Clinical Neurosciences, 20*(4), 315–336. https://doi.org/10.1111/j.1440-1819.1966.tb02646.x

Kawai, H. (2008). *Buddhism and the art of psychotherapy*. Texas University Press.

Krech, G. (2022a). *Naikan: Gratitude, grace, and the Japanese art of self-reflection*. Stone Bridge Press.

Krech, G. (2022b). *Naikan therapy, Tricycle*. Retrieved May 23, 2023, from https://tricycle.org/magazine/naikan-therapy/

Kwee, M. G. (2015). *Buddhist psychotherapy, Academia.edu*. Retrieved July 26, 2023, from https://www.academia.edu/16770118/Buddhist_Psychotherapy

Lambert, M. J., & Okiishi, J. C. (1997). The effects of the individual psychotherapist and implications for future research. *Clinical Psychology: Science and Practice, 4*(1), 66–75. https://doi.org/10.1111/j.1468-2850.1997.tb00100.x

Lilienfeld, S. O., & Arkowitz, H. (2012). Are all psychotherapies created equal? *Scientific American Mind, 23*(4), 68–69. https://doi.org/10.1038/scientificamericanmind0912-68

Magid, B. (2002). *Ordinary mind: Exploring the common ground of zen and psychoanalysis*. Wisdom Publications.

Magid, B. (2008). *Ending the pursuit of happiness*. Wisdom Publications.

Magid, B. (2013). *Nothing is hidden: The psychology of Zen koans*. Wisdom Publications.

Masson, J. M. (1988). *Against therapy: Emotional tyranny and the myth of psychological healing*. Atheneum.

Mathers, D., Miller, M. E., & Ando, O. (2009). *Self and no-self: Continuing the dialogue between Buddhism and psychotherapy*. Routledge.

McLynn, F. (1998). *Carl Gustav Jung*. St. Martin's Griffin.

Meckel, D. J., Moore, R. L., & Abe, M. (1992). The self in Jung and Zen. In *Self and liberation. The Jung-Buddhism Dialogue* (p. 128). Paulist Press.

Morita, S., & Morita, S. (1998). *Morita therapy and the true nature of anxiety based disorders (Shinkeishitsu)*. State Univ. of New York Press.

Nakamura, K. (2013). *A disability of the Soul: An ethnography of schizophrenia and mental illness in contemporary Japan*. Cornell University Press.

Onfray, M. (2011). *Le crépuscule d'une idole: L'affabulation freudienne*. Librairie générale française.

Popper, K. (1992). Science: Conjectures and refutations. In *Philosophy of science and the occult* (pp. 87–93). State Univ. of New York Press.
Reynolds, D. K. (1989). *Flowing bridges, quiet waters: Japanese psychotherapies, morita and Naikan*. State University of New York Press.
Ricks, D. F. (1974). Supershrink: Methods of a therapist judged successful on the basis of adult outcomes of adolescent patients. In *Life history research in psychopathology* (pp. 275–297). University of Minnesota Press.
Rosenzweig, S. (1936). Some implicit common factors in diverse methods of psychotherapy. *American Journal of Orthopsychiatry, 6*(3), 412–415. https://doi.org/10.1111/j.1939-0025.1936.tb05248.x
Rubin, J. B. (2013). *Psychotherapy and Buddhism: Toward an integration*. Springer Science + Business Media, LLC.
Shedler, J. (2011). The efficacy of psychodynamic psychotherapy. *Psychodynamic Psychotherapy Research*, 9–25. https://doi.org/10.1007/978-1-60761-792-1_2
Silva, C. O. (2007). Demystifying Japanese therapy: An analysis of naikan and the AJASE complex through Buddhist thought. *Ethos, 35*(4), 411–446. https://doi.org/10.1525/eth.2007.35.4.411
Silva, C. O.-D. (2009). *Psychotherapy and religion in Japan: The Japanese introspection practice of Naikan*. Routledge.
Steinert, C., et al. (2017). Psychodynamic therapy: As efficacious as other empirically supported treatments? A meta-analysis testing equivalence of outcomes. *American Journal of Psychiatry, 174*(10), 943–953. https://doi.org/10.1176/appi.ajp.2017.17010057
Suzuki, D. T. (1964). *An introduction to Zen Buddhism/with a foreword by C.G. Jung*. Grove Press.
Tomio Hiray (1927–1993). (n.d.). *Tomio Hiray*. Retrieved July 24, 2023, from https://terebess.hu/zen/mesterek/HiraiTomio.html
Wampold, B. E. (2015). How important are the common factors in psychotherapy? An update. *World Psychiatry, 14*(3), 270–277. https://doi.org/10.1002/wps.20238
Wampold, B. E., & Imel, Z. E. (2015). *The great psychotherapy debate: The evidence for what makes psychotherapy work*. Routledge.
Wampold, B. E., et al. (1997). A meta-analysis of outcome studies comparing bona fide psychotherapies: Empirically, "All must have prizes.". *Psychological Bulletin, 122*(3), 203–215. https://doi.org/10.1037/0033-2909.122.3.203
Watters, E., & Healy, D. (2011). The mega-marketing of depression in Japan. In *Crazy like us: The globalization of the American psyche* (pp. 168–220). Free Press.

Watts, A. W. (1963). *Psychotherapy, East and West*. Pantheon.
Welwood, J. (1983). *Awakening the heart*. Boulder.
Welwood, J. (2002). *Toward a psychology of awakening: Buddhism, psychotherapy, and the path of personal and spiritual transformation*. Shambhala.
Wu, H., et al. (2015). Morita therapy for anxiety disorders in adults. *Cochrane Database of Systematic Reviews* [Preprint]. https://doi.org/10.1002/14651858.cd008619.pub2
Yampolsky, P. B. (1971). *The Zen master Hakuin: Selected writings*. Columbia UP.
Young-Eisendrath, P., & Muramoto, S. (2003a). *Awakening and insight Zen Buddhism and psychotherapy*. Taylor and Francis.
Young-Eisendrath, P., & Muramoto, S. (2003b). The Jung-Hisamatsu conversation. In *Awakening and insight Zen Buddhism and psychotherapy* (p. 112). Taylor and Francis.
Zweig, S. (1969). *Mental healers: Franz Anton Mesmer, Mary Baker Eddy, Sigmund Freud*. Frederick Ungar Publ. Co.

6

The Mind and the Natural World: Buddhism, Science and the Reality of Reality

Many species of living organisms populate the Earth: countless animals and plants that have changed subtly from their ancestors through an endlessly long and continuous process of evolution. This world of living beings is enormous not only in its variety but also in its complex and reciprocal interconnectedness: the network of links between each individual, its group, its species and its environment. It was the mutual interconnectedness of this network which, in the 1970s, led James Lovelock to formulate his 'Gaia hypothesis', in which he proposed that living organisms and their inorganic surroundings form a synergistic and self-regulating complex system that sustains life on the planet (Lovelock, 2016).

From this complex system, approximately 300,000 years ago, a species called *homo sapiens* emerged in Africa. Since then, it has gradually spread to almost all of the surface of the planet, reaching a global population of over eight billion as of the beginning of the twentieth century. The human species has some characteristics of the great apes, while it is also largely hairless, bipedal and with opposable thumbs. It is endowed with remarkably large brains that confer upon it high intelligence and cognitive skills, which reached their modern stage of development about 160,000–60,000 years ago. The species' unique feature seems indeed to

T. Giraldi, *Zen Buddhism and the Reality of Suffering*,
https://doi.org/10.1007/978-3-031-69244-4_6

be the size and complex structure of the brain, with millions and millions of brain cells (neurons), each of which communicates with the others through approximately 1000 connections (synapses). It is the complex intricacy of this extraordinary organ that permits the equally complex functions of human mind, such as social behaviour, intellectual curiosity and motivation to understand and influence phenomena. And these, in turn, have developed into myriad forms of conceptual fields, from mythology, religion and philosophy to science, technology and others.

The modern brain and its functions are extremely complex and varied, and that variety is represented by the chapter titles of the concise guidebook, *The Brain: A User's Guide,* which covers: *Perception, Intelligence, Consciousness' and 'The Unconscious, Thinking, Memory, Learning, The Self, Creativity, Decision Making, The Social Brain, Sleep and Dreaming'* and *Brain Disorders* (*The Brain: A User's Guide*, 2018). A similarly concise compendium of the progress of neuroscience, which focuses particularly on themes such as perception and action, cognition and emotions, is *30-Second Brain. The 50 Most Mind-Blowing Ideas in Neuroscience, Each Explained in Half a Minute* (Seth & Hissey, 2018).

The unique richness of the brain allowed knowledge to be transmitted and accumulated, while humans' basic genetic structure has remained largely unchanged since the appearance of *homo sapiens.* The memes, as proposed by Dawkins and Blackmore, may have cooperated with these biological processes for shaping the human mind and culture (Dawkins, 2016a, 2016b; Blackmore & Dawkins, 2000).

Human history shows the development of human society with its notable positive and negative consequences: it must not be overlooked that collective social phenomena are still the result of distinct individuals' actions. A question which cannot therefore be eluded is that of the individual self, the entity with which every person identifies his subjectivity, which determines their actions and upon which the representation of the inner and outer world depends. Each individual has their own stable and at the same time dynamic beliefs about what they consider reality, depending on a variety of factors, such as their biological constitution, the previous experiences and the beliefs and decisions they have drawn.

The self is generally not felt to be distinct from an individual's mind and body, while it does not correspond to a specific unitary anatomical or physiological entity. From a biological perspective, the collective functions of the mind-body complex are involved in preserving the individual and permitting reproduction by maintaining optimal internal conditions and adapting to external environmental challenges. All of these functions are subjected to the pressure of natural sexual selection to ensure that the best genes transmitted to the progeny promote the survival and expansion of the species.

When we consider humans as naked apes forged by evolution, it is clear that this has been driven by the nervous system and particularly the brain. The individual's relationship with the external world depends on the perceptions and sensations provided by the sense organs, which are processed by the brain.

Given the complexity of the brain and the amazing amount of sensory information continuously received, it is easy to see why it needs to be processed without the subject's full, conscious cognizance. Our cognitive awareness is fed a model of the external and internal world, which the brain constantly produces and updates.

From an evolutionary perspective, this mechanism might seem to be a limitation for the individual, when the collective level of the species is considered; however, it is an extremely successful evolutionary tool. In the neurosciences, this mechanism has been dubbed *the predictive mind*, a hypothesis-testing machine that governs our actions by using the evidence provided by the senses to steadily minimise the errors in its predictions. The concept is remarkably simple and is supported by strong theoretical arguments: it is conceivable that it might be extended to include the very notion of consciousness itself (Hohwy, 2014).

The human mind is thus expected to optimise the behaviour of the individual, who at the same time may be largely unaware of the limitations of the model of reality presented by the brain. This affects the entirety of mental activity, including the consciousness of what is happening around and the capacity to make choices. The brain's mental representation of the external and internal world is therefore made by mechanisms that have been investigated by both psychology and the neurosciences. Some of these have been mentioned above, but we must also not forget the vast amount of previous experiences which are hidden in the unconscious and which, together with the emotions, determine a large part of our mental activity.

Seen in this light, the highly valued self, which many take to wholly represent their individuality, is merely a function of the brain, which controls every feeling, thought and action based on the total of individual experiences accumulated in the person's life, and which resurface from moment to moment as a fragmentary consciousness.

Individual human activity is entirely subject to these mechanisms, and the true process through which our brain creates its representation of the inner and outer worlds is inaccessible to our subjective intentional consciousness. What each individual identifies with their self and the external and internal world is only a construct of the brain's model of reality, which it is continuously evolving and from which only fragments reach our conscious mind.

This natural, constitutional inability to directly comprehend reality makes it difficult for us to distinguish between the glimpses of our brain's modelling that are supplied to us and other spontaneous products of the mind such as dreams, delusions, illusions and hallucinations. The picture is further complicated by cultural factors such as the passive acceptance of superstitions and beliefs that characterise our societies.

In relatively recent human history, certain developments enabled a degree of liberation from some of these constraints and allowed a somewhat more direct engagement with the reality of the natural world. One of these, in Western Europe, was the seventeenth and eighteenth century 'Age of Enlightenment' also known as the 'Age of Reason'. The values which powerfully and irreversibly emerged were based on the pursuit of knowledge obtained through reason and the evidence of the senses, together with ideals such as natural law, liberty, progress, toleration, fraternity, constitutional government and separation of church and state. Science, scientific advancement, empiricism and rational thinking played a major role in the 'Age of Enlightenment', substantially contributing to the overthrow of religion and traditional authority in favour of the development of free thought and speech (Zafirofski, 2014).

These radical innovations constituted the beginning of the era of progress which continues until our present time. The factor which might be regarded as crucial for the progress of humankind is a new and more direct relationship with the natural world. Myths and superstitions were replaced by theories which could be tested empirically, and whose soundness could be determined with objective, shared observation and reproducibility. The efficacy of the objective scientific method for understanding the natural world is clearly shown by the success of the applications that have radically transformed our society. They have enabled such effective control and exploitation of the natural world that during our lifetime, they even threaten the survival of that same natural order on our planet.

The empirical understanding of the human mind, however, has posed different challenges. The human body has been analysed in detail, from its overall anatomy down to its underlying genetic and molecular structure; the isolated and coordinated functions of the organs have been similarly explained by physiology. The structure of the nervous system, of the brain and its peripheral and vegetative parts, as well as their basic mechanisms, have also been traced with success. The higher functions of the brain have been studied by philosophers and psychologists, and the essence and working of the human psyche and mind have puzzled the greatest thinkers. Most recently, through the neurosciences, it has become possible to attempt a more detailed, scientific analysis of the brain. Basic questions about life and human nature, however, remain without satisfactory answers; a full understanding of the human mind remains as elusive as ever, from the complexity of the brain's functions to the fleeting nature of the individual self.

There is an extremely broad body of literature offering contributions on these questions. A prominent example is Chris Frith's *Making Up the Mind: How the Brain Creates Our Mental World.* The title clearly states the goal, which Frith presents with clarity and concision. Frith is a Professor in Neuropsychology at the Wellcome Trust Centre for Neuroimaging at University College London UK, and in the prologue of his book, he recalls how during his career he often felt uneasy because of the gap between psychology, which was traditionally regarded as a more subjective soft science, and the objectivity of the hard scientific approach made possible by the progresses in the neurosciences. Frith's experiences are particularly interesting because as a psychologist by training, he has been actively involved in using new brain imaging technologies, such as the functional magnetic resonance (fMRI), to study the higher brain functions. His experimental work and his books have been positively received and praised by highly esteemed figures, including Oliver Sacks and Vilayanur Subramanian Ramachandran, both well-known for their contributions on similar subjects. Incisively covering a range of important themes, *Making Up the Mind* concludes with a final chapter simply called *The evidence*, which details the experimental evidence and the publications that support Frith's arguments. The structure of the book highlights the range of challenges involved in attempting to understand the nature of the individual self, as well as the relationship of the self to the individual internal and external world (Frith, 2013).

The first part of Frith's book, *Seeing Through the Brain's Illusions*, stresses how everything we know about the physical and mental world comes to our cognizance through the mediation of our brain. Our relationship with the physical world of objects is no more direct than our brain's connection with the mental world of ideas; the existence of direct contact with objects in the physical world is just an illusion created by our brain.

Examples of the evidence supporting this view are numerous and strong. There are neurological conditions in which a person with a physical or psychological disability is cognitively unaware of being affected by it, a disorder which has been named *anosognosia*. This and similar conditions can result from physical damage to brain structures and are sometimes accompanied by *asomatognosia*, a form of neglect in which patients deny ownership of body parts such as their limbs. A variation of *anosognosia* is the 'phantom limb' sensation which frequently occurs in amputee subjects, who may feel very strongly that the missing limb is still part of their body. These remarkable conditions have been engagingly described by Ramachandran in *Phantoms in the Brain: Probing the Mysteries of the Human Mind* (Ramachandran & Blakeslee, 2009). There are similarly vivid descriptions of clinical cases in Sachs' *The Man Who Mistook His Wife for a Hat and Other Clinical Tales* (Sacks, 1998).

There is further evidence to be found in illusions, where a perception seems to be different to reality and which are attributed to defects in the brain's processing. There is extensive research on illusions, and one area that deserves special consideration is that of the visual illusions that arise because of the brain's mis-processing of some classes of objects. The phenomenon occurs so frequently that it has even inspired artists, such as M.C. Escher, with fascinating results (Shapiro & Todorović, 2016).

Our brains' continuous efforts to coherently represent the internal and external world to our conscious mind can be thrown off course not only by the distortions of visual illusions but can even extend to our brains producing sensory and cognitive impressions independent of external reality.

Physiologically, one clear example is our dreams, which are believed to have a profound relationship to our mental well-being. Sometimes manifesting as nightmares, their content may in some instances be retrieved while awake and may provide a glimpse of the internal workings of our mind, conveyed in the 'language' of the unconscious. When recalled, the contents of dreams and nightmares can be as vivid as real experiences.

Most people experience illusions and distortions of the senses and, hence, of their perception of reality. Some people, however, experience more serious psychiatric disorders such as delirium, hallucinations and delusions. Hallucinations occur despite there being no external stimulus present, whereas illusions consist of a distortion or misrepresentation of true sensory experience. Delirium, meanwhile, is a complex combination of symptoms observed in psychiatry, including drowsiness, agitation, disorientation, or hallucinations accompanied by acute disturbances in attention, awareness and global cognition.

Delusions are a key theme in psychiatry, but despite their frequency and potential severity, descriptions of them are often hazy. They are commonly defined as a false fixed belief that persists in spite of conflicting evidence, although there is widely recognised difficulty in distinguishing between delusions and strongly held ideas. Delusions are reported to occur in some physical diseases and mental disorders; they are believed to be a key symptom of psychotic conditions such as schizophrenia, bipolar disorders and psychotic depression (Persaud, 2003; Bortolotti, 2018; Bell et al., 2003).

There is much additional evidence about how the brain creates false knowledge. Frith recalls a number of classic cases where subjects suffering from epilepsy experience vivid and complex visual hallucinations during seizures. Oliver Sacks has also contributed significantly to the subject of hallucinations with a number of classic, brightly reported cases (Sacks, 2013).

Similarly compelling are reports by the Canadian neurosurgeon Wilder Penfield, about operations performed on patients suffering from serious epilepsy, where surgery was the only effective treatment available. During open skull interventions, direct electrical stimulation of the brain surface was used to get information about the functioning of the particular areas being operated on. The conscious patients reported extremely vivid experiences, very similar to the hallucinations they experienced during seizures.

One related point is that using minute dosages of some hallucinogenic compounds like lysergic acid diethylamide (LSD) can cause profound and long-lasting disruption to the brain's perception and representation of the internal and external world (Frith, 2013). There is a great variety of naturally originating substances which, since pre-historic times, have been known to have a range of profound effects on the brain, and in later times, new synthetic chemical compounds have been added to the list. These substances' actions are so varied that many have unexpectedly aided in the study of the brain's mechanisms and higher functions, and this deserves more detailed consideration.

Some officinal plants contain poisonous active ingredients, and the study of these toxic substances contributed to understanding the functioning of the brain; empirical evidence shows that in some cases, they could be used, at appropriate dosages, as useful medicines. Most of these substances are known from the past and include alcohol, the opium alkaloids, cannabis, cocaine and nicotine. They directly affect the coordinated functioning of the brain cells, markedly modifying the mental functions. In some cases, they even induce addictive dependence in chronic users, accompanied by severe withdrawal symptoms.

The hallucinogenic and psychedelic compounds cause more profound and subtle effects on the brain and mental activity. Hallucinogens produce profound alterations in perception, thought and mood, which are accompanied by altered states of consciousness. Psychedelics are a specific subgroup which induces additional alterations in mental activity and consciousness similar to those reported during religious, spiritual, mystical and meditative transcendental experiences. Healers and shamans employed the psychedelic effects of mescaline and psilocybin long before the West turned to them for recreational and investigational purposes.

When considering psychotropic agents, it is possible to precisely and objectively describe their properties by studying their somatic and neurological effects. These are described clearly in medical texts, like *Julien's Primer of Drug Action: A Comprehensive Guide to the Actions, Uses, and Side Effects of Psychoactive Drugs* (Julien et al., 2023). There are also academic articles clearly and scientifically describing their histories, properties and mechanisms of action (Mehling, 2004; Nichols, 2004).

This objective perspective, however, does not fully show all of the complex effects caused by hallucinogens and psychedelics, which are markedly different from those of the traditional psychotropic substances. The literature available on their effects on higher mental functions is varied and largely of an anecdotal, subjective nature. This suggests that psychedelics involve profound human experiences, with subjective states of disrupted self-consciousness accompanied by 'self-loss' and 'ego dissolution' somewhat similar to what is believed to occur during meditation (Millière et al., 2018). Psilocibin in particular has been reported to induce mystical-type experiences claimed to have great personal meaning and spiritual significance (Griffiths et al., 2006; Stoliker et al., 2021). Psychedelics have also been shown to cause the near-death experiences that commonly accompany ego-dissolution and mystical states (Timmermann et al., 2018). One conclusion that many have drawn is that since psychedelic drugs reduce or abolish the sense of a distinct self or 'I', their effects can be considered direct evidence for the non-existence of the individual self (Letheby & Gerrans, 2017).

Many shamanic and other ritual practices have long involved naturally occurring psychedelic compounds (Metzner, 1998). The 1960s and 70s counterculture movement in the USA and beyond, however, also explored these properties. A new movement called the 'psychedelic era' began, inspiring the musical, social, artistic and intellectual worlds, including many famous personalities. LSD also attracted the attention of psychiatry, and researchers suggested using it to study and treat mental diseases (Dyck, 2008). As part of this, it has recently been proposed to use psilocibin and ketamine, a dissociative anaesthetic with hallucinogenic side effects, to treat depression (De Gregorio et al., 2020).

Psychedelics thus seem to be closely connected to the realm of religiosity, spirituality, mysticism and consciousness. In this form, they appear to have accompanied human culture throughout its history, as described in Ellens' *Seeking the Sacred with Psychoactive Substances: Chemical Paths to Spirituality and to God* (Ellens, 2014).

There are many brilliant and important contributions on this subject, including Aldous Huxley's *Doors of Perception*, *Heaven and Hell* and *Moksha,* which include prefaces by both Albert Hoffman, the 'father' of LSD, and Alexander Shulgin, who was later widely known as a 'psychonaut' because of his promotion of psychotropic drugs (Huxley, 2013; Huxley et al., 2007; Hofmann, 2009). Timothy Leary is another key figure who became widely known for his various experimental uses of LSD, and in 1964, he reported some of his studies in a book entitled *The Psychedelic Experience: A Manual Based on the Tibetan Book of the Dead.* Dedicated to Aldous Huxley, this work argues that the psychedelic experiences have traits in common with those described in the old Buddhist Tibetan scriptures (Leary et al., 2008).

The effects of substances, particularly psychedelics, on the functioning of the brain strongly suggest the fragility and evasiveness of a 'real', individual self, since it can be disrupted and even transformed by even minute amounts of psychedelic drugs. They also suggest a deeply ingrained cluster of beliefs, partly cultural, partly possibly involving constitutive genetic and somatic traits, which may be the basis for the innate tendency towards religiosity, spirituality, mysticism and likely also consciousness and free will.

Throughout history, across cultures and religious traditions, psychoactive substances have been used to facilitate visionary, mystical and spiritual experiences. This involved a wide variety of naturally occurring substances which, with appropriate dosage and modality of use, could affect the brain's higher mental functions, alongside their prevalent and more characteristic somatic physiological effects (Ott, 1996). In more recent times, the term 'entheogens' has been proposed for the broad range of psychedelic hallucinogenic compounds, such as psilocibin, peyote and LSD (Ellens, 2014; Leeming et al., 2010). One peculiar example which perhaps deserves specific consideration is that of *ayahuasca*, a concoction that some South American indigenous cultures traditionally used for its healing properties for mental and physical ailments as well as for spiritual ceremonies; it is an ingenious brew, whose pharmacological properties have only recently been understood. It is prepared using indigenous plants containing DMT, a hallucinogen which is naturally present in the mammalian brain at low concentration, together with some plant alkaloids which strongly enhance its action. Ayahuasca causes significant effects in the nervous system, including mystical and spiritual experiences (Ruffel et al., 2023). These profound experiences prompted the foundation in 1961 of the Brazilian religious society, the *União do Vegetal*, in which sacred rites are based on the consumption of ayahuasca (União do Vegetal, 2023).

It is worth noting that Buddhism appears to have been aware of the effects of psychotropic substances on the brain and hence on the whole person, and recommended the avoidance of intoxicating substances; this was formalised as the precepts of the Buddhist schools and traditions.

Much of what has been considered thus far in this chapter has been formalised by Andrew Newberg into a single framework which he has termed 'neurotheology'. In *Why God Won't Go Away: Brain Science and the Biology of Belief*, Newberg and his collaborators consider religion, transcendence, the idea of God and the need to create beliefs, in relation to the brain's mechanisms and how it determines the reality of human experience (Newberg et al., 2002). In *Neurotheology: How Science Can Enlighten Us About Spirituality*, Newberg analyses in more depth how our self is constricted within the boundaries of our brain, with its predisposition to create myths, rituals, as well as religious and spiritual practices. Newberg also gives careful consideration to the relationship between neurotheology and psychology, and how mental pathologies can affect religious ideas and experiences. He refers to the abundant literature about the religious delusions frequently observed in schizophrenic subjects and the intense religious experiences which occur in patients with temporal lobe epilepsy. He also explores the changes in religious attitudes which are observed after brain damage or surgical intervention, in the course of neurodegenerative diseases, and after near-death experiences (Newberg, 2021).

The mind's properties and attributes depend on the structure and function of the brain, which is the phenotypic manifestation of the genetic information which shapes our body and its organs. The question then arises whether individual genetic differences, called genetic polymorphism, may influence our mind and its propensity to spirituality; this

> has been investigated by Dean Hamer, a well-respected geneticist. In his book *The God Gene. How Our Faith Is Hardwired into Our Genes,* Hamer reports the results of his studies into individual genetic variations of one poorly investigated biochemical feature of the brain cells, the vesicular monoamine transporter, VMAT2. He concludes that genetic polymorphism leads to altered biochemical functionality and can indeed influence individual inclination towards mysticism (Hamer, 2005).

So far, we have explored naturalistic, phenomenological and objective evidence for the relationship between the human brain and the mind. Overall, we can begin to see how human evolution shaped us in such a way that at any one time, our individual cognitive awareness can only access a limited mental representation of the internal and external world. The brain selects a minute part of what it has processed of the external world, the overall extent of which would otherwise be unmanageable for us. The vast majority of the brain's processes are unconscious and in parts of the mind that we cannot actively access. The unavoidable inference is that we have no direct contact with internal and external reality but only with fragments of the representation our mind produces of it. A further consequence is that even the most valued individual higher mental functions, be it in metaphysics, religiosity, spirituality or mysticism, are still part of this representation.

Particular attention can be given to Buddhism here. It is indeed regarded as one of the great religions, because of its long history dating back to the discourses and teachings of Siddhartha Gautama, the historic Buddha, in Northern India in the fifth century BC. Buddhism then spread to a large proportion of Asia, becoming the fourth largest religion, with over half a billion followers worldwide today.

Buddhism has some traits in common with other great faiths, such as Judaism, Christianity and Islam. In temples and shrines, for instance, Buddhist monks and priests administer rites and rituals, providing religious services to the population. On the other hand, Buddhism radically differs from these Abrahamic religions since it does not make any reference to supernatural spheres and divinities. It does not refer to faith, revelations and scriptures believed to originate from God's words and does not consider concepts of holiness and sacredness to matters of faith. The essence of the Buddhist teachings is the indication of a way towards the cessation of the existential sufferings which accompany life. Devoid of most of the trappings of other religions, Buddhism is instead considered a philosophy. The Buddha is represented as a typical human being, who has reached liberation from life's suffering through awakening, and he is presented just as one of the Buddhas which have existed (Smith & Whitaker, 2016).

Buddhism focuses on the human mind and the existential sufferings that occur in the course of life with clarity and simplicity. Its scriptures also extensively and comprehensively explore the idea of reality as a product of the ordinary human mind. The aim of the practice is enlightenment, awakening a clear mind free of attachments, constrictions and limitations, and liberation from the illusions and delusions which unfailingly accompany life experiences. In the centuries of its diffusion from Northern India to Asia, Buddhism became integrated into different local cultures, adapting to different traditions, at the same time, retaining its core values and message. Among the enormous size of transcribed Buddhist teachings, there are a few central, unifying themes that will be explored here.

The three Marks of existence, impermanence and emptiness (*anicca*), non-self, selflessness (*anatta*) and Suffering (*dukkha)*, characterise human life. The individual's attachments, through the mind's flawed perception of ever-changing reality, lead to the existential ailments of life.

The sufferings of human life can be understood and overcome by selflessly following The Four Noble Truths: Suffering, Origin of Suffering, Cessation of Suffering, and the Eightfold Noble Path, the Middle Way.

The principles of the Eightfold Noble Path, Wisdom, Morality and Meditation, are the Way leading to awakening, the enlightenment that brings the individual outside the limitation and constraints of the ordinary, un-awakened mind. The Middle Way can be seen as a natural path towards the physiological mental state of enlightenment, beyond individual identification with all the experiences and beliefs stored in the ordinary mind. A further focus point, which appears in the Buddha's Discourse to the Kalamas, is the need for unremitting experiential, experimental and moral consideration of life events based on full individual responsibility.

Meditation appears in the Eightfold Noble Path, together with Wisdom and Morality, as characterised by three attributes: Right Effort, Right Awareness (*sati*) and Right Concentration (*samadhi*). It has a central place in the rich complexity of Buddhist teachings. Meditation is the focal point of the Hinayana Theravada discourses *Satipatthana* and *Anapanasati Sutta*. The central importance of meditation is laid out even more explicitly in the Mahayana tradition of Zen. Zazen, the Deep Concentration of the *shikantaza* of Soto school, is presented as leading towards awakening. The Rinzai Zen school relies additionally on *koans* to achieve a direct, sudden realisation of the *kensho,* which is verified in individual interviews (*dokusan* and *sanzen*) between the disciple and the master, the Roshi: further practice may then deepen the *kensho* and *satori* experiences.

Traditional Zen monasteries have the aim of leading disciples to *kensho* and *satori*, the capacity to free oneself from the limitations of the ordinary mind and acquire direct, deliberate access to the internal and external worlds.

In monasteries, Zen has been a living presence for centuries, where uninterrupted lineages of masters transmitted their experience to the next generation of monks. Zen monk training to become a Zen master is very demanding. During their training, monks have to study several collections of traditional koans, such as the *Mumonkan*, *Hekigan Roku* and *Rinzai Roku*. The training requires permanent residence in a training monastery with a recognised master, and the challenges are enormous, especially for Westerners who face not only the innate difficulties but also language and culture barriers. The average time required to be recognised as a master is measurable in tens of years, usually between 20 or even 30 (Sharf, 1995a, 1995b). The history and organisation of the Rinzai Zen is described in detail by Borup (Borup, 2008). The practice of koan study is even more complex, and there is much literature dealing with *koans*, *kensho* and *satori*, as well as enlightenment.

These crucial subjects have been approached by several authors. These include Daisetz T. Suzuki's *The Zen Koan as a Means of Attaining Enlightenment* (Suzuki, 1994), as well as Miura and Sasaki, with works including *The History of the Koan in Rinzai (Linji) Zen* and *The Koan Study in Rinzai Zen* in *Zen Dust* (Miura & Sasaki, 2015a, 2015b). Koan study is also considered from various perspectives in *Sitting with Koans*, edited by John D. Loori with an introduction by Thomas Yuho Kirchner. Koans are still studied, though with less emphasis, to accompany the practice of the deep meditation *shikantaza* in the Soto Zen school (Loori, 2012).

Interesting contributions have also been made about the use of koans and the current state of Rinzai Zen in Japan by Jeff Shore, a fully traditionally trained Zen master of American origin, who is also a faculty member of Hanazono University in Kyoto (Shore, 1996, 2017). Barry Magid has argued for a psychological approach to unite the practice of koans with contemporary psychotherapy (Magid, 2013).

It was, indeed, interest in lay practice that inspired Bankei Yotaku, a great master in the seventeenth century. His teachings were simply expressed, easy to understand, and attracted large audiences. He became popular for his originality and the simplicity of his teachings, which centred on the concept of the *unborn*, which was accessible for the general population. Regrettably, he did not initiate his own lineage (Bankei & Waddell, 2000).

The great master Hakuin Ekaku repeatedly addressed the question of the study of koans, and some of his writings are collected in *Hakuin on Kensho: The Four Ways of Knowing* (Low, 2006). He successfully introduced a reform to revitalise Zen practice and created a koan curriculum which had to be 'passed' in a precise sequence; their study began with one of three koans which are called the *kensho koan*. The first of the *Mumonkan* is probably the best known: 'A monk asked Joshu, has a dog the Buddha Nature? Joshu answered Mu'. To successfully 'pass', the disciple is required to provide the master with a demonstration of the grasp of Zen obtained with meditation, and this is called as 'Passing through the Gateless Gate':

> Arouse your entire body with its three hundred and sixty bones and joints and its eighty-four thousand pores of the skin; summon up a spirit of great

> doubt and concentrate on this word 'Mu.' Carry it continuously day and night. Do not form a nihilistic conception of vacancy, or a relative conception of 'has' or 'has not.' It will be just as if you swallow a red-hot iron ball, which you cannot spit out even if you try. All the illusory ideas and delusive thoughts accumulated up to the present will be exterminated, and when the time comes, internal and external will be spontaneously united. You will know this, but for yourself only, like a dumb man who has had a dream. Then all of a sudden an explosive conversion will occur, and you will astonish the heavens and shake the earth.
>
> It will be as if you snatch away the great sword of the valiant general Kan'u and hold it in your hand. When you meet the Buddha, you kill him; when you meet the Patriarchs, you kill them. On the brink of life and death, you command perfect freedom; among the sixfold worlds and four modes of existence, you enjoy a merry and playful samadhi (Sekida et al., 2005).

The experience of *kensho* is described in a dramatic way here, and there is a vast accompanying literature of other episodes and stories, some historic and others presumably symbolic. They are all largely anecdotal, aiming to describe the indescribable experience of awakening through the experiences of learners faced by the puzzling paradoxes of Zen and the master's teachings.

Robert Sharf, in his essay *Buddhist Modernism and the Rhetoric of the Meditative Experience,* challenges the historical picture that individuals have to experience a new, specific state of consciousness during meditation. He argues that the role of these experiences has been exaggerated in contemporary scholarship, particularly through Western amplifications of certain twentieth-century Asian reform movements which are strongly focused on Zazen and Vipassana meditation (Sharf, 1995a, 1995b).

From these examples, we can clearly see the complexity of koan study, the effort and time needed to proceed through it. In this context, it is understandable that the difficulties for laypeople have led to several modern attempts to make these practices more accessible. Jeff Shore's *A Buddhist Model of The Human Self: Working Through the Jung-Hisamatsu Discussion* recalls Hisamatsu's proposal to use only one fundamental koan. Hisamatsu has been involved in making the practice of Zen more accessible to contemporary followers, and he helped to establish

F.A.S. Society, where 'F' stands for the *Formless self*, 'A' for taking the standpoint of *All humankind*, and 'S' for creating *Suprahistorical history*. Hisamatsu created a fundamental koan: 'As I am, however I am, will not do. Now what do I do?' The study of koans through regular encounters with the master was replaced with a sort of group encounter, called *mutual enquiry* (Shore, 2002; Ives, 2010). Michio Ochi described his personal experience with Hisamatsu and the F.A.S., and pointed out the basic similarities between *mutual enquiry* and group counselling and psychotherapies. Surprisingly, he explicitly refers to *Transactional Analysis* (TA), pointing to the similarity of existential questions like 'Am I good to myself?', to ensuing TA propositions: 'I'm OK, you're not OK', 'You're OK, I'm not OK', 'I'm not OK, you're not OK', 'I'm OK, you're OK', and considering this in relation to *mutual enquiry* (Ochi, 1997).

In an attempt to make Zen practice less severe and lengthy for trainees and to adapt it to modern times and the needs of lay followers, in 1954, Yasutani Hakuun Roshi founded the *Sanbokyodan* movement. It significantly diverges from the demanding training in Soto, Rinzai and Obaku monasteries and temples. The use of koans is retained but shorter and simplified, yet the attainment of *kensho* remains central (Sharf, 1995a, 1995b).

A traditional graphical depiction, accompanied by succinct verses, which may be very useful for a lay beginner on the path to enlightenment, is *Ten Ox herding Pictures*. Several editions have been made, which have been commented on in the past by great Zen masters, such as Yamada Mumon Roshi, showing their past and present great value (Yamada & Hori, 2004).

Buddhism remains in various Eastern cultures where it was adopted early on. It has recently moved to Western cultures such as in America and Europe, where it has set down roots in new environments. Buddhism's movement to the West is occurring against the backdrop of an increasingly global society. Globalisation is profoundly challenging in many senses, as the speed of transportation and communication is transforming many aspects of human existence. New life events and challenges in coping with them have arisen, accompanied by new existential sufferings. Buddhism's core message is universal and can also be applied to the challenges of the modern age. We can expect that it will continue to adapt to the changes occurring in East and West, although it remains difficult to imagine how past traditions will adapt to society and the individual needs of the future.

Zen and Rinzai Zen, with their directness and essentialism, may have an active role in this process. This, however, may raise new challenges. The questions have been asked if there are any longer the great masters seen in the past and how alive is Zen not only in the West but even in Japan. In America and Europe, the teachers available now are Westerners belonging to new lineages of Dharma transmission, residing in the new monasteries and temples they established in the West.

The modern world has brought unexpected developments. Science offered itself as alternative means to Buddhism to comprehend nature and alleviate the sufferings of life. Psychology, and later the neurosciences and biological psychiatry, attempted to progress with the exploration of the human brain and mind, and its manipulation. In this context, a new movement was even founded, 'mindfulness', a poorly defined archipelago spanning from the purest Buddhist traditions to materialistic commercial 'spiritual capitalism' for the treatment of existential sufferings, with questionable theoretical grounding. The following chapters will examine these contemporary developments.

References

Bankei, & Waddell, N. (2000). *The unborn: The life and teachings of Zen master Bankei, 1622–1693*. North Point Press.

Bell, V., Hallighan, P., & Ellis, H. (2003). Beliefs about delusions. *The Psychologist, 16*(8), 418–423.

Blackmore, S., & Dawkins, R. (2000). *The meme machine*. Oxford University Press.

Bortolotti, L. (2018). *Delusions in context*. Palgrave Macmillan.

Borup, J. (2008). *Japanese Rinzai Zen Buddhism myōshinji, a living religion*. Brill.

Dawkins, R. (2016a). *The blind watchmaker: Why the evidence of evolution reveals a universe without design*. Penguin Books.

Dawkins, R. (2016b). *The selfish gene*. Oxford University Press.

De Gregorio, D., et al. (2020). Hallucinogens in mental health: Preclinical and clinical studies on LSD, psilocybin, MDMA, and ketamine. *The Journal of Neuroscience, 41*(5), 891–900. https://doi.org/10.1523/jneurosci.1659-20.2020

Dyck, E. (2008). *Psychedelic psychiatry: LSD from clinic to campus*. Johns Hopkins University Press.

Ellens, J. H. (2014). *Seeking the sacred with psychoactive substances: Chemical paths to spirituality and to God*. Praeger.

Frith, C. (2013). *Making up the mind: How the brain creates our mental world*. Wiley.

Griffiths, R. R., et al. (2006). Psilocybin can occasion mystical-type experiences having substantial and sustained personal meaning and spiritual significance. *Psychopharmacology, 187*(3), 268–283. https://doi.org/10.1007/s00213-006-0457-5

Hamer, D. (2005). *The God gene: How faith is hardwired into our genes*. Anchor Books.

Hofmann, A. (2009). *LSD, my problem child: Reflections on sacred drugs, mysticism, and science*. MAPS, Multidisciplinary Association for Psychedelic Studies.

Hohwy, J. (2014). *The predictive mind*. Oxford University Press.

Huxley, A. (2013). *The doors of perception; Heaven and hell*. Important Books.

Huxley, A., et al. (2007). *Moksha*. Edhasa.

Ives, C. (2010). True person, formless self: Lay Zen master Hisamatsu Shin'ichi. In *Zen masters* (pp. 218–239). Oxford University Press.

Julien, R. M., Advokat, C. D., & Comaty, J. E. (2023). *Julien's primer of drug action: A comprehensive guide to the actions, uses, and side effects of psychoactive drugs*. Worth Publishers.

Leary, T. F., Metzner, R., & Dass, R. (2008). *The psychedelic experience a manual based on the Tibetan Book of the Dead*. Penguin Books.

Leeming, D. A., et al. (2010). Entheogens. In *Encyclopedia of psychology and religion*. Springer.

Letheby, C., & Gerrans, P. (2017). Self unbound: Ego dissolution in psychedelic experience. *Neuroscience of Consciousness, 2017*(1). https://doi.org/10.1093/nc/nix016

Loori, J. D. (2012). *Sitting with Koans: Essential writings on Zen Koan introspection*. Wisdom Publications.

Lovelock, J. (2016). *Gaia: A new look at life on Earth*. Oxford University Press.

Low, A. (2006). *Hakuin on kensho: The four ways of knowing*. Shambhala.

Magid, B. (2013). *Nothing is hidden: The psychology of zen koans*. Wisdom Publications.

Mehling, R. (2004). *Hallucinogens*. Chelsea House.

Metzner, R. (1998). Hallucinogenic drugs and plants in psychotherapy and shamanism. *Journal of Psychoactive Drugs, 30*(4), 333–341. https://doi.org/10.1080/02791072.1998.10399709

Millière, R., et al. (2018). Psychedelics, meditation, and self-consciousness. *Frontiers in Psychology, 9*. https://doi.org/10.3389/fpsyg.2018.01475

Miura, I., & Sasaki, R. F. (2015a). Koan study in Rinzai Zen. In *Zen dust: The history of the Koan and Koan study in Rinzai (Linji) Zen* (pp. 31–70). Melbourne University, VIC: Quirin Press.

Miura, I., & Sasaki, R. F. (2015b). The history of the Koan in Rinzai (Linji) Zen. In *Zen dust: The history of the Koan and Koan study in Rinzai (Linji) Zen* (pp. 3–30). Melbourne University, VIC: Quirin Press.

New Scientist. (2018). *The brain: A user's guide*. John Murray.

Newberg, A. B. (2021). *Neurotheology: How science can enlighten us about spirituality*. Columbia University Press.

Newberg, A. B., D'Aquili, E. G., & Rause, V. (2002). *Why God won't go away: Brain science and the biology of belief*. Ballantine Books.

Nichols, D. E. (2004). Hallucinogens. *Pharmacology & Therapeutics, 101*(2), 131–181. https://doi.org/10.1016/j.pharmthera.2003.11.002

Ochi, M. (1997). The fundamental Koan and mutual inquiry: My own experience and views. *F.A.S. Society Journal 96: The Fundamental Koan and Mutual Inquiry*. Retrieved October 9, 2023, from http://www.fas.x0.com/writings/fasj/fj96kihonkoane.html

Ott, J. (1996). *Pharmacotheon: Entheogenic drugs, their plant sources and history*. Natural Products.

Persaud, R. (2003). *From the edge of the couch: Bizarre psychiatric cases and what they teach us about ourselves*. Bantam Press.

Ramachandran, V. S., & Blakeslee, S. (2009). *Phantoms in the brain: Probing the mysteries of the human mind*. Harper Perennial.

Ruffel, S., et al. (2023). *Ayahuasca—A review of historical, pharmacological, and therapeutic aspects*. Psyarxiv.com. Retrieved September 21, 2023, from https://psyarxiv.com/7h48b/

Sacks, O. (1998). *The Man Who Mistook his wife for a hat and other clinical tales*. Simon & Schuster.

Sacks, O. (2013). *Hallucinations*. Picador.

Sekida, K., et al. (2005). *Two Zen classics: The gateless gate and the Blue Cliff Records*. Shambhala.

Seth, A. K., & Hissey, I. (2018). *30-Second brain: The 50 most mind-blowing ideas in neuroscience, each explained in half a minute*. Icon Books Ltd.

Shapiro, A. G., & Todorović, D. (2016). *The Oxford compendium of visual illusions*. Oxford University Press.

Sharf, R. (1995a). Buddhist modernism and the rhetoric of meditative experience. *Numen, 42*(3), 228–283. https://doi.org/10.1163/1568527952598549

Sharf, R. H. (1995b). Sanbōkyōdan: Zen and the way of the new religions. *Japanese Journal of Religious Studies, 22*(3–4). https://doi.org/10.18874/jjrs.22.3-4.1995.417-458

Shore, J. (1996). *Koan Zen from the inside*. Retrieved October 5, 2023, from https://terebess.hu/zen/mesterek/koan-zen.pdf

Shore, J. (2002). A Buddhist model of the human self. Working through the Jung-Hisamatsu discussion. In *Awakening and insight: Zen Buddhism and psychotherapy* (pp. 29–42). Brunner-Routledge.

Shore, J. (2017). *Rinzai Zen now*. Retrieved October 5, 2023, from https://beingwithoutself.files.wordpress.com/2016/08/rinzai-zen-now.pdf

Smith, D., & Whitaker, J. (2016). Reading the Buddha as a philosopher. *Philosophy East and West, 66*(2), 515–538. https://doi.org/10.1353/pew.2016.0026

Stoliker, D., et al. (2021). *Effective connectivity of LSD-induced ego dissolution* [Preprint]. https://doi.org/10.1101/2021.12.28.21268391

Suzuki, D. T. (1994). *The Zen koan as a means of attaining enlightenment*. C.E. Tuttle Co.

Timmermann, C., et al. (2018). DMT models the near-death experience. *Frontiers in Psychology, 9*. https://doi.org/10.3389/fpsyg.2018.01424

União do Vegetal. (2023). *Centro Espírita Beneficente União do Vegetal*. Retrieved September 21, 2023, from https://udv.org.br/en/

Yamada, M., & Hori, V. S. (2004). *Lectures on the ten oxherding pictures*. University of Hawai'i Press.

Zafirofski, M. (2014). *Enlightenment and its effects on modern society*. Springer.

7

Science and the Natural World: The Puzzle of Complex Nonlinear and Chaotic Phenomena

Among all the great variety of creatures living today, humankind has accomplished an enormous array of achievements. Mammals, as all other animals, can be seen as a product of Darwinian evolution. Each species is the result of random genetic mutations being passed on, and some new traits enable individuals to better adapt to their environment and cope with the challenges to survival. Over time, these environmental pressures led these traits to be naturally selected for genetic transmission in a dynamic, continual process which led to the astonishingly rich diversity of creatures alive today.

The evolution of the human species has been characterised above all by the development of the nervous system and the brain in particular. The human brain is composed of a uniquely large number of nervous cells (neurons), and even more functional connections (synapses) between the neurons. It is the amazingly complex structure of the human brain that has given this species exceptional capacities to manipulate the natural world: the sophistication of the human brain is unequalled by any other animal species.

From the earliest available historical evidence, the humans' basic genetic traits have been substantially stable until the present day. On the

T. Giraldi, *Zen Buddhism and the Reality of Suffering*,
https://doi.org/10.1007/978-3-031-69244-4_7

other hand, that time has been marked by the appearance of structured social groups of increasing size and complexity. A crucial event in the development of human society is the sudden appearance of modern science. Beginning in the seventeenth and eighteenth centuries, the Age of Enlightenment, also known as the Age of Reason, produced radical innovations in the understanding of the natural world. This led to the beginnings of modern science, which through a new *scientific method*, enabled thought to advance from the speculative conceptual frames of the past and thus progressively relinquish the superstitions and philosophical representations of natural phenomena which had reigned until that time.

The scientific method, generally attributed to Galileo Galilei, is based on rigorous scepticism and the careful observation of natural phenomena. It enables hypotheses to be made, which are tested with evidence from experiments designed to test the reproducibility of results with independent observers, and to establish cause-effect relationships.

The consequences are dramatic. The knowledge of natural phenomena, freed from the restrictions of faith, superstition and untestable philosophical abstractions, enabled rapid advancements and technological development. Scientific progress led to extremely detailed and comprehensive understanding of the natural world. This knowledge was also used for practical applications and industrial development, the successes of which are in themselves a powerful demonstration of the potential of the scientific method (Shimony, 1993a, 1993b).

It has to be remembered that these events came about because of individuals whose rational advances still occurred through the mechanisms of the mind: the individual self's production of a representation of the internal and external world, which may be subject to the fallacies explored in previous chapters. It is therefore not surprising that the continuous flow of scientific progress has sometimes been interrupted by instances in which exciting findings that were initially applauded were later shown to be based on false observations and theories which were then discarded.

One notable case in physics was the supposed discovery of *N rays* at the beginning of the twentieth century by a recognised scientific researcher from the University of Nancy, Prosper-René Blondlot. His initial observation in 1903 was immediately confirmed by almost 300 articles published by more than 100 reputable scientists, until in 1905, the American physicist Robert W. Wood showed beyond any doubt that N rays do not exist and were based on subjective, incorrect analysis. This episode became a classic cautionary tale about the scientific errors which can be caused by the observer's biases (Lagemann, 1977).

Even the highly respected Nobel Foundation was involved in similar cases, having awarded prizes for discoveries which were subsequently shown to be wrong. One notable example was when the prize for Medicine and Physiology was given in 1925 to Johannes Fibiger for his discovery of the *Spiroptera carcinoma*, also called *Gongylonema neoplasticum*, a parasite of rats and insects, which was proposed as the cause of cancer in rodents. These findings were later shown to be false, and the case is considered one of the biggest blunders ever made by the Karolinska Institute. Moreover, the 1927 Nobel Prize was awarded to Julius Wagner-Jauregg 'for his discovery of the therapeutic value of malaria inoculation for the treatment of dementia paralytica'. It was immediately and enthusiastically used by psychiatrists before being shown to be substantially ineffective and dangerous for patients. An even more shocking case is the award of the 1949 Nobel Prize to Egas Monitz 'for his discovery of the therapeutic value of leucotomy in certain psychoses'. Leucotomy, also known as lobotomy, is a surgical intervention on the brain; after a period of initial enthusiasm, it was soon abandoned as it was shown to be totally ineffective and to cause extremely severe and irreversible damage to patients (Nobel Prizes in Physiology and Medicine, 2023).

The unique ability of the scientific method to provide new knowledge and even control the physical world is clear. Its crucial value lies in its ability to correct the mistakes that occur because of the errors that can arise because of researchers' subjectivity and abstract speculation, however sophisticated. False findings can be subsequently corrected thanks to researchers' collective cooperation and through the use of an approach proposed by Karl Popper. Indeed, the best thinkers have devoted their efforts to the problems of science and scientific knowledge, and it is worth explaining Popper's contributions in particular, along with the wider work of the philosophy of science. In *The Logic of Scientific Discovery*, Popper proposed that there is a logic asymmetry between verification and falsifiability and that only falsifiability was a valid criterion for genuine science. A theory, possibly drawn by experimental observations, could be considered scientific if, and only if, it is falsifiable: a new, radical and sophisticated perspective (Popper, 1992). As an example, on these grounds, he criticised generally accepted assumptions about the scientific status of psychoanalysis and Marxism, because neither can be tested for falsifiability. It is worth noting that he does not indulge in considering the vast range of philosophic approaches to reality, conjectures and science. As he sets out in *Objective Knowledge: An Evolutionary Approach* and *Conjectures and Refutations: The Growth of Scientific Knowledge*, he does not care whether a conjecture or theory is based on observations of the natural world, or a thought experiment or even a dream; in the end, it just has to stand experimental tests and a falsifiability verification. This is the reason why Popper openly regarded Albert Einstein as one of the greatest scientists, whose theory of relativity after long heated debates was experimentally validated according to falsifiability by later astronomical observations (Popper, 1972, 2021).

Qualitative observations were universally used until, at the end of the nineteenth century, Ronald Aylmer Fisher developed a new approach to statistical sciences. One of its basic propositions is to test hypotheses through the specific design of experiments, the results of which must be subjected to mathematical testing. It thus became possible to analyse the probability that the initial hypothesis was wrongly verified by chance, because of the limited size of the experimental groups, and thus reject it. Methods such as the *analysis of variance*, and concepts like the significance of the differences in mean values in various experimental groups, became universally accepted and were further developed. Experiments based on these principles came to be widely accepted in medicine and psychology and led to the development of clinical trials using evidence-based approaches, which are now the 'gold standard' for objective, reproducible results (Box, 1979).

The current widely accepted means of assessing the validity of scientific findings is to publish them in a scientific journal after a thorough *peer review*. This requires that every new and original scientific report be evaluated by anonymous reviewers. Only with their agreement may the new finding be accepted for publication in a scientific journal of the best reputation, thus becoming available to the scientific community, where it can be accepted and critiqued. Peer reviewing is a means of validating new findings, and attempting to avoid the reporting of false findings, which, as we have seen, was not uncommon before. As might be expected, however, this innovation can also cause inconveniences. The Nobel Prize laureate Randy Shekman complained that a sort of tyranny could thus be exercised by the top scientific journals, negatively influencing scientific research and communication. In 2013, he publicly declared a boycott on publishing in top journals such as *Nature, Cell* and *Science* (The Guardian, 2013).

There are also cases of deliberate scientific hoaxes, orchestrated to call attention to the limitations of the peer review system when it is not subjected to the test of experimental falsification, for example, in fields such as theoretical physics. An article in *The New Scientist* details some of the known cases (Harris, 2016). One interesting example is that of Alan Sokal, who in 1996 decided to test whether a fully invented nonsensical article could be accepted for publication in a journal of high repute. The article was based on meaningless fantasies, similar to the journal's average contents, sounding good but riddled with evidently fantastical statements. It was accepted for publication by a leading North American journal of cultural studies, the board of which included eminent scientific personalities. The article, *Transgressing the Boundaries: Towards a Transformative Hermeneutics of Quantum Gravity*, was published, causing great embarrassment for the journal when it was later revealed that it was a deliberate hoax, leading to a fierce debate (Sokal, 2010). Sokal's initiative gained a certain notoriety and the support of highly regarded scientists. Sokal later widened his focus, publishing a book whose title summarises his concerns: *Fashionable Nonsense: Postmodern Intellectuals' Abuse of Science*. His concerns are mainly to do with the often impenetrable lingo of contemporary thinkers and theorists, and the irrational misunderstandings that can give unproven and untenable arguments a façade of scientific respectability. Sokal gives several examples to support his views and shows how the humanities are particularly vulnerable to abstruse communication and almost undecipherable jargon; Jacques Lacan is the first example considered in his analysis (Sokal & Bricmont, 1999).

The scientific understanding of the physical world has progressed extraordinarily, thanks to the scientific method and an unprecedented number of active researchers. The natural world has now been traced in comprehensive detail, from subatomic particles to the huge size of the universe and from the briefest physical and chemical occurrences to the genesis and history of the universe.

It has been asked whether this progress in the natural sciences can continue without end. A related question is about the validity of the scientific method, which has been so successful for understanding the physical world and developing technologies, for understanding the metaphysical realm of the human psyche and its manifestations.

One person who has provided an informed perspective on the future of scientific research is John Maddox, a physicist by training who held important scientific positions and was the editor of *Nature*, the prestigious British scientific journal, for 22 years from 1966 to 1995 (Gratzer, 2010). In 1999, he published *What Remains to be Discovered: Mapping the Secrets of the Universe, the Origins of Life, and the Future of the Human Race*, in which he showed, based on his unique experience at the helm of *Nature*, the new discoveries in areas such as physics, biology, health and intelligence, which he believed would only accelerate in future (Maddox, 1999).

A completely different image of the future of science appears in the work of John Horgan. Not a scientist as Maddox was, but a full-time staff writer for *Scientific American* from 1986, he received many professional awards for his writing, also at other prestigious publications. In 1997, however, the journal fired him over a dispute about his first book, the 1996 *The End of Science: Facing the Limits of Knowledge in the Twilight of the Scientific Age* (John Horgan, 2023).

The contents of this book are rich and complex, and it is not surprising that they led to heated controversies. To make his case, Horgan interviewed scientific luminaries who had made outstanding discoveries in specific fields, a unique, vivid and realistic approach which includes these individuals' first-hand perspectives about their contributions. Horgan also used this method, with brilliant and challenging results, for his later books, *The Undiscovered Mind: How the Human Brain Defies Replication,*

Medication, and Explanation (Horgan, 2000) and *Rational Mysticism: Spirituality Meets Science in the Search for Enlightenment* (Horgan, 2004).

In the *End of Science*, Horgan argues that pure science, defined as 'the primordial human quest to understand the universe and our place in it', may continue but experience a progressive decline. He suggests that insights into nature as profound as evolution through natural selection, the DNA double helix, the Big Bang, relativity theory or quantum mechanics are unlikely to occur in future. His argument is that science will refine, extend and apply these concepts but that further great revolutions or revelations are highly improbable. His interviews with people such as Stephen Hawking, Francis Crick and Richard Dawkins lead him to conclude that all the big questions have already been answered and that modern approaches, such as string theory, have a nature he defines as 'ironic' and 'theological', since they are impossible to confirm experimentally and cannot therefore be held to be scientific.

The scientific method has led to the extraordinary advances in our objective knowledge of the physical world which have accompanied the development of human culture in the last couple of centuries. These same successes have, however, shown the limitation of the scientific method when it moves from simple to complex phenomena. Some examples may help to clarify this point.

Human communities have been affected by many illnesses, with serious or even potentially disastrous consequences. Diseases like rickets, scurvy and anaemia were endemic, and plague and other epidemics could decimate entire populations. No really effective intervention was possible while the only available explanations were those provided by faith, superstition and abstract speculation. With the appearance of scientific approaches, however, these unsubstantiated beliefs were progressively replaced by objective understanding of the mechanisms behind these conditions, which allowed scientists to identify effective remedies. For instance, rickets were found to be caused by lack of vitamin D; scurvy by lack of vitamin C; and anaemia by lack of iron. These conditions were responsive to treatment through correction of the deficiency. Similarly, plague and other epidemics were shown to be caused by pathogenic infectious microorganisms and could be controlled by adequate hygienic measures and vaccination.

These approaches succeeded because they involve isolated, 'simple' phenomena, where a single main cause, like paucity of a defined factor, is responsible for the problem. This can then be attenuated and may even disappear, when the deficit is corrected. The evidence shows a clear, proportional cause-effect relationship for the efficacy of the remedy. Science could thus successfully progress with the identification of the natural phenomena where a single main direct cause-effect could be identified.

At the same time, however, scientific progress seems to have now reached a stage where it must deal with problems for which a single main cause cannot be identified. There is also evidence that in many cases, natural evolution has led to the appearance of delicate systems characterised by structural complexity. Complex systems may be seen as an articulated network of concurring factors which cooperate and share peculiar resilience to external interfering influences.

Various attempts have been made to address the problems arising from complexity. It is outside the aim of this chapter to analyse them in detail, but some points will be recalled because of their relevance to the progress of the natural physical sciences and for the accompanying metaphysical challenges such as the understanding of the human mind.

Complexity in this context has been defined as the behaviour of a system whose components interact in multiple ways and cause non-linearity and apparent randomness in the behaviour of the phenomenon considered (Heylighen et al., 2011).

The study of complexity is associated with *chaos theory*. Researchers in this field focus on the deterministic laws of dynamical systems that are highly sensitive to initial conditions and whose successive states appear to be characterised by randomness, disorder and irregularities. This happens because of the mathematical nonlinear properties of complex systems' responses to variations in initial conditions. Just a small change can result in large differences at a later stage, with the additional consequence that long-term predictions are generally impossible (Bird, 2003; Lorenz, 2008).

Another related concept is that of *fractals*. Fractals are strongly dependent on precise mathematical factors, and even experts do not agree on a simple definition. The initiator of studies in this field, Benoit Mandelbrot, described fractals as 'a rough or fragmented geometric shape that can be split into parts, each of which is a reduced-size copy of the whole'. Besides their geometric and graphical appearance, the underlying mathematical principles are involved in the complexity of numerous natural phenomena, and in particular, they significantly contribute to biological and physiological processes (Mandelbrot, 2021).

Scientists' research is now yielding an unprecedented number of results. Scientific progress has been possible thanks to the inherent advantage of scientific method ability to reject previous false findings. Communication of results using the peer review system has also played its part. Whatever the cause, what we have been accumulating is true understanding of an incredible number of natural phenomena.

Interesting work has been done on these subjects by Bruce J. West, a senior research scientist at Duke University and Army Research in the USA, who defines himself as interested in the nonlinear interactions and the resulting emergent properties of social, biological, or physical phenomena. His concerns clearly appear in the title of his book *Where Medicine Went Wrong. Rediscovering the Path to Complexity*. The chapters of this book deal with themes such as *Even Uncertainty has Laws, Randomness and measurement, Chaos and determinism, Fractal Physiology, Controlling complexity, Disease as loss of control and of complexity*. This book appeared in the series *Studies of Nonlinear in Life Sciences Phenomena,* edited by West, which includes 16 other volumes on topics such as *Fractal Physiology and Chaos in Medicine, Nonlinear Dynamics in Human Behavior, The Complex Matters of the Mind,* and *Autonomous Agents: Nonlinear Systems Approaches to Cognitive Psychology and Cognitive Science* (West, 2006).

West's contributions align with the issues raised by Horgan in *The End of Science*, as well as with those raised in Franklin's *What Science Knows, and How It Knows It* (Franklin, 2009). Scientific exploration of the natural world may now have reached a level of sophistication where the intrinsic limitations of traditional, conventional approaches mean they may no longer be able to deliver progress.

Concerns have also been raised about the validity of scientific results gained using traditional approaches to medical research. Previously, evidence-based methods, together with adequate statistical analysis, enabled the reporting of effective and repeatable observations. Over time, however, there has been greater need to be cautious about the design of protocols. Even when the so-called *gold standard* appeared, the random double-blind design including placebo, the results obtained still largely depended on initial choices like the criteria for selecting patients and evaluating efficacy and safety. Similar concerns have increasingly been raised about the methods and criteria for statistical analysis.

An article called *Why Most Published Research Findings Are False* was published in 2005 by John P. A. Ioannidis in the excellent journal, *PLoS Medicine*. Ioannidis' aim was to prove that in clinical medicine, most research findings are false despite the accepted scientific procedures used. Based on mathematical reasoning, he proposed and identified a number of factors leading to biases in current protocols and analysis (Ioannidis, 2005).

What can be summarised briefly here is that despite the apparent soundness of the methods used, and the acceptance of the scientific community through peer review evaluation, there is a widening gap between the formal reliability of new findings and their limited meaning when critically analysed and applied in general practice.

One key factor is a misunderstanding of the meaning of statistical analysis and in particular the so-called *statistical significance* of data. In their book *The Cult of Statistical Significance: How the Standard Error Costs Us Jobs, Justice, and Lives*, Ziliak and McCloskey stress how the meaning of statistical analysis has been transformed since its initially effective principles and applications. The authors consider medicine and a variety of other fields from agronomy to zoology, where statistical significance was originally used to ascertain the probability that an observed event was occurring because of a cause-effect relationship and not by chance. The value of statistical significance has come to be used to mean the relevance of the observation, independent of its magnitude and its real significance, after its occurrence has been statistically validated (Ziliak & McCloskey, 2014).

These are some of the substantial challenges to the study of the natural world. The progress of science in the Age of Reason and its successful use to understand the physical world opened the way for its application to understand the human mind and the metaphysical questions associated with it. There is an additional challenge here, because when the mind is studied, it is unavoidably the case that the subject of the study is the same tool used to study it, with all the limitations associated with the representation of the inner and outer world that we have seen.

The study of the mind had historically been closely related to philosophy and religion. However, when the rational experimental methods which had been so effective in the study of the natural world were applied to the human psyche and behaviour, radical innovations became possible. Researchers were able to proceed beyond the realm of abstract thought and speculation, which, in spite of its sophistication, was not amenable to objective shared evaluation, and to definite validation or confutation. Thus, the new field of experimental psychology developed, the aim of which was to apply the scientific method to understanding the human mind and its behaviour.

Initially, this field developed along several lines. First, innovative physiological methods were applied to the study of perception and bodily reactions to perceived stimuli, opening up an important path. It also became possible to critically and experimentally challenge the psychic phenomena which were extremely popular at the end of the nineteenth century, such as extrasensory perception, telepathy, precognition, clairvoyance, psychokinesis and apparitional experiences. By and large, these were essentially shown to be fraudulent and based on the beliefs and misled perceptions of the subjects (Randi & Asimov, 1980; Alcock, 1990).

Psychology could thus begin in earnest to study the mind and behaviour, in order to understand mental processes such as thoughts, feelings and behaviours, at conscious and unconscious levels. New disciplines were founded, with behaviourist, cognitive, psychoanalytic, existential humanist, interpersonal, social and biological evolutionistic focuses. New methods of investigation were also devised for the physiological approach, such as psychometric questionnaires and quantitative measures, followed by sophisticated statistical analysis of the results (Wertheimer & Puente, 2020).

These developments enabled remarkable advances in the study of the human mental processes in both the psychological sciences and psychotherapies. At the same time, two clearly divergent approaches began to emerge, which would affect all later developments in this area.

In the first, the foundations of psychoanalytic thought paved the way for the psychodynamic approach, with its existential, humanist, personal and interpersonal characteristics. In this approach, the existential sufferings are caused by real or imaginary traumas which may be hidden in the subject's subconscious, causing *neurotic conditions*. The insights obtained through analysis may work to counteract the consequences of these conditions. These principles formed the basis for the development of person-centred humanist psychotherapies. In these fields, quantitative assessments are avoided in favour of qualitative and narrative methods. The human elements involved in general simply do not allow for rigorous, objective testing, and these approaches have sometimes been criticised for being anecdotal and unscientific as a result.

In this context, it is worth considering the concept of *insight*. When this was studied in Gestalt psychology, it was defined as the solution to a problem which has not been solved by the subject after several deliberate attempts but which suddenly presents itself to them without warning. The potential relevance for the understanding of the human mind is clear, and this concept has also been examined in relation to the psychiatric and spiritual elements of Buddhist meditation (Sternberg, 2002; Sayadaw, 2016).

The analogies with the practice of *koans* in Zen, and the sudden realisation of *kensho* and *satori*, are strongly suggestive. Awakening, enlightenment, kensho and satori are central aspects of the Middle Way and Buddhist practice, and their analogy to psychological insight is apparent. This is worth exploring not only from a speculative perspective but also to examine what may be a natural state of consciousness. The nature of this state is not yet clearly understood and deserves to be examined more closely, with modern procedures more sophisticated than those used in the past by Tomio Hirai (Hirai, 1989).

The second type of approach that developed is more biological in nature, originating from the examination of conditioning reflexes in a behaviourist framework. Later, these would develop into cognitive approaches, which were accompanied by the appearance of cognitive and behavioural therapies. This field also thrived based on advances in the neurosciences.

Progress in these cognitive approaches was largely based on diagnostic and psychometric methods, which allowed for quantitative evaluation of a subject's psychological ailments and the results obtained from cognitive-behavioural interventions. The field would also adopt and benefit from technological advances in the neurosciences, such as brain images obtained using scanning techniques and even analysis of individual genetic polymorphism. It shared these developments with the new field of *biological psychiatry*, which also implemented cognitivism with its cognitive-behavioural psychotherapies.

The psychodynamic view that existential sufferings have a neurotic origin disappeared, and was replaced by the definition of a large number of *mental disorders*, based on the identification of a constellation of symptoms in a subject that did not appear in the average population, without consideration of the subject's reaction to life events. This was realised with the American Psychiatric Association's *Diagnostic and Statistical Manual of Mental Disorders*, which, after its first edition in 1952, became the basic tool for the diagnosis of mental ailments. Even normal, healthy mood changes arising from coping with distressing life events thus became mental disorders. The manual has come to be used by psychiatrists and clinical psychologists using cognitive-behavioural approaches; at the same time, however, it has also been subject to serious criticisms (Giraldi, 2017). In essence, the problems arise from the attempt to describe the human mind reductively, in spite of the complexity and variety of human experiences.

The huge number of scientific reports accumulating to defend these approaches mainly focus on isolated observations of small groups and areas of research. Overall, these efforts towards scientific objectivity do not appear to have created an effective framework for the properties and functioning of the mind. It is perhaps not surprising that these approaches have been charged with oversimplification and mechanistic reductionism.

It may be appropriate at this stage to recall what Buddhism has said about the understanding of the physical world and the human mind. It must be remembered that the breadth of Buddhist scriptures is immense. The original texts available now are collections made throughout several councils over the centuries, written in Pali and Sanskrit. These have only been recently translated, with great effort, into English. To do this and correctly render the core message of Buddhism from Pali and Sanskrit, specific vocabularies had to be developed (Humphreys, 1952). The concepts we are dealing with here are the central and highly complex themes of Buddhism, so it will only be possible to remind the reader of them now in an extremely succinct way.

According to Carl Gustav Jung, psychology and Buddhism have in common the goal of addressing the mental and existential suffering encountered in life. The radical difference between their two approaches is that psychology aims to act on the individual self, whereas Buddhism considers the individual self to be an illusion produced by the ordinary mind. According to the Buddha's teachings, it is possible to comprehend the phenomena of the natural world and the human mind by following the Four Bodhisattva's Vows, understanding the Four Noble Truths and progressing along the Eightfold Noble Path (the Middle Way), towards enlightenment.

The mind is at the centre of Buddhism: the existential suffering that necessarily accompanies human life can be overcome through enlightenment and liberation from the illusion of individual selfhood, leading to the release from the endless fluctuations of internal and external reality.

In Buddhism, this framework is presented simply, clearly and with implicit certainty. Each individual is invited to leave behind beliefs, faith and teachers, to abstain from logic, inference and speculation, and is encouraged to a moral exploration of its existence.

Buddhist teachings are complex and varied but are expressed clearly, comprehensively and concisely, and the *Heart Sutra*, which is revered and regularly chanted in the Mahayana tradition, is an example. The key elements involved are the Three Marks of Existence, the Three Jewels, the Three Poisons and the Precepts.

Meditation, wisdom and morality are essential and are clearly illustrated in two of the Buddha's discourses, the *Anapanasati Sutta* (The Breath Awareness Discourse) and the *Satipatthana Sutta* (The Great Discourse on the Establishing of Awareness). These include detailed instructions for using the breath as the focus for meditation, together with descriptions of the challenges and hindrances that can arise and the elements on the path to awakening.

Buddhism also contains the doctrine of Dependent Origination, or Dependent Arising, which presents all phenomena, physical and mental, as arising from mutual interdependence with all other phenomena (Buddhadasa Bhikkhu, 1978). This notion indirectly addresses the problems encountered in the scientific examination of phenomena whose relationships cannot be reduced to simple cause-effect, leading to complexity and unpredictability.

The Five Factors of Clinging, material and mental, are also relevant here. These are form, sensations, perceptions, discrimination and consciousness. Their combination is what constitutes a sentient being's person and personality, and these therefore contribute to their attachments and suffering. There has always been substantial interest in the concept of consciousness, for example recently with the eminent philosopher Daniel C. Dennett's book *Consciousness Explained* (Dennett, 2007). In recent years, the field of neuroscience has advanced substantially and focused its attention on this question, and it has come to be seen as one of the great and most baffling scientific challenges. Its nature remains elusive, and it is debated whether it could ever be comprehensively understood (Zelazo et al., 2007). It is worth noting that in Buddhism, consciousness is plainly one of the senses, the Five Factors whose combination creates the person.

The rich variety of these traditional Buddhist teachings is presented comprehensively in the *Bhavachakra*, the Wheel of Life, in order to make them more accessible to devotees of different traditions. The fierce figure holding the wheel represents impermanence, the moon above the wheel represents liberation from the constant cycles of existence, and the Buddha shows that liberation from life's sufferings is possible.

The Buddhist representation of the internal and external individual world can be regarded as one of humanity's most valuable creations, and in spite of being 2500 years old, it remains as existentially compelling as ever today.

On the one hand, the doctrine of Dependent Origin shows the futility of detailed concentration on individual factors for explaining the entirety of the various phenomena. On the other hand, the Buddhist vision of the mind and nature explains how the existential and mental sufferings unavoidably accompany human existence.

There are clear implications from this for the challenges the sciences face in developing knowledge of and intervention in the physical world. There are also clear implications for the challenges arising from the *soft sciences* attempts to understand the human mind through psychology, as well as the *hard sciences* attempts to do the same through neuroscience.

Although Buddhism developed and thrived in the East for more than two millennia, in the last two centuries, it has begun its journey West. During this process, although the traditions of many different schools, such as Hinayana Theravada, Mahayana Tibetan and Zen, largely survived the translation, something unexpected happened in the late 1990s when a new approach called *mindfulness* began to emerge. The intention was to introduce 'Buddhist meditation without Buddhism' as an intervention to treat mental ailments caused by stress (Giraldi, 2020). This idea developed at an amazing pace and became widely popular; how this happened, and the characteristics of this new Western approach to meditation and mental suffering, will be explored in the next chapter.

References

Alcock, J. E. (1990). *Science and Supernature: A critical appraisal of parapsychology*. Prometheus Books.

Bird, R. J. (2003). *Chaos and life: Complexity and order in evolution and thought.* Columbia Univ. Press.

Box, J. F. (1979). *R. A. Fisher: The life of a scientist.* Wiley.

Buddhadasa Bhikkhu. (1978). *Principle of dependent origination.* Buddhadasa Bhikkhu—Paticcasamuppada: Practical Dependent Origination. Retrieved January 8, 2024, from https://www.dhammatalks.net/Books6/Bhikkhu_Buddhadasa_Paticcasamuppada.htm

Dennett, D. C. (2007). *Consciousness explained.* Back Bay Books, Little, Brown.

Franklin, J. (2009). *What science knows and how it knows it.* Encounter Books.

Giraldi, T. (2017). *Unhappiness, sadness and 'depression': Antidepressants and a mental disorder epidemic.* Palgrave Macmillan.

Giraldi, T. (2020). *Psychotherapy, mindfulness and Buddhist meditation.* Palgrave Macmillan.

Gratzer, W. (2010). Sir John Royden Maddox. 27 November 1925–12 April 2009. *Biographical Memoirs of Fellows of the Royal Society, 56*, 237–255. https://doi.org/10.1098/rsbm.2009.0024

Harris, E. (2016). Eleven of the greatest scientific hoaxes. *New Scientist.* Retrieved December 22, 2023, from https://www.newscientist.com/article/dn15012-eleven-of-the-greatest-scientific-hoaxes/

Heylighen, F., Bollen, J., & Riegler, A. (2011). The growth of structural and functional complexity during evolution. In *The evolution of complexity* (pp. 17–44). Springer.
Hirai, T. (1989). *Zen meditation and psychotherapy*. Japan Publ.
Horgan, J. (2000). *The undiscovered mind: How the human brain defies replication, medication, and explanation*. Touchstone.
Horgan, J. (2004). *Rational mysticism: Spirituality meets science in the search for enlightenment*. Houghton Mifflin.
Humphreys, C. (1952). *Buddhism*. Middlesex, Penguin Books.
Ioannidis, J. P. (2005). Why most published research findings are false. *PLoS Medicine, 2*(8), e124. https://doi.org/10.1371/journal.pmed.0020124
John Horgan. (2023). *John Horgan (The Science Writer)*. Retrieved December 23, 2023, from https://johnhorgan.org/about-john-horgan
Lagemann, R. T. (1977). New light on old rays: N rays. *American Journal of Physics, 45*(3), 281–284. https://doi.org/10.1119/1.10643
Lorenz, E. N. (2008). *The essence of chaos*. Univ. of Washington Press.
Maddox, J. (1999). *What remains to be discovered: Mapping the secrets of the Universe, the origins of life, and the future of the human race*. Papermac.
Mandelbrot, B. B. (2021). *The fractal geometry of nature*. Echo Point Books & Media.
Nobel Prizes in Physiology and Medicine. (2023). NobelPrize.org. Retrieved December 14, 2023, from https://www.nobelprize.org/prizes/lists/all-nobel-laureates-in-physiology-or-medicine/
Popper, K. R. (1972). *Objective knowledge: An evolutionary approach*. Clarendon Press.
Popper, K. R. (1992). *The logic of Scientific Discovery*. Routledge.
Popper, K. R. (2021). *Conjectures and refutations: The growth of scientific knowledge*. Hassell Street Press.
Randi, J., & Asimov, I. (1980). *Flim flam!: The truth about unicorns, parapsychology, and other delusions*. Lippincott & Crowell.
Sayadaw, M. (2016). *Manual of insight*. Wisdom Publications.
Shimony, A. (1993a). Search for a naturalistic world view. In *Natural science and metaphysics*. Cambridge University Press.
Shimony, A. (1993b). *In Search for a naturalistic world view. Scientific method and epistemology*. Cambridge University Press.
Sokal, A. (2010). *Beyond the hoax: Science, philosophy and culture*. Oxford University Press.

Sokal, A. D., & Bricmont, J. (1999). *Fashionable nonsense: Postmodern intellectuals' abuse of science*. Picador USA.

Sternberg, R. J. (2002). *The nature of Insight*. MIT Press.

The Guardian. (2013). *Peer review and scientific publishing. Nobel winner declares boycott of Top Science Journals*. Retrieved December 22, 2023, from https://www.theguardian.com/science/2013/dec/09/nobel-winner-boycott-science-journals

Wertheimer, M., & Puente, A. E. (2020). *A brief history of psychology*. Routledge.

West, B. J. (2006). *Where medicine went wrong: Rediscovering the path to complexity: Studies of nonlinear phenomena in life sciences*. https://doi.org/10.1142/9789812773098 Publisher: World Scientific.

Zelazo, P. D., Moscovitch, M., & Thompson, E. (2007). *The Cambridge handbook of consciousness*. University Press.

Ziliak, S. T., & McCloskey, D. N. (2014). *The cult of statistical significance: How the standard error costs us jobs, justice, and lives*. The University of Michigan Press.

8

Mindfulness East and West, Cognitive Therapies and Biological Psychiatry

Throughout its long history, Buddhism has spread from its origins in Northern India to China, other Asian countries and beyond. In the process, it became firmly rooted in the culture of the new areas to which it spread, adapting to local traditions with radically different external forms, while maintaining the same core message and values. Two thousand years later, Buddhism entered a new stage when it began to spread to Western cultures, establishing at the end of the nineteenth century a firm foothold in North America and Europe especially in the British Empire. The basic principles of the schools, the Mahayana Zen, the Hinayana Theravada, and later the Vajrayana following the exile of Tibetans to Northern India and to other Western countries, were still preserved, in spite of the dramatically different new cultural environments.

The continuity of the teaching was achieved by transmission through the lineages of masters living in established temples and institutions. Their place within these institutions also allowed them to satisfy the religious needs of the local lay population. Modern studies of Buddhism suggest that one of the key purposes of Buddhist monastic practice, and meditation in particular, was to induce mystical experiences in the minds of monks and to produce the specific discrete 'states of consciousness'

T. Giraldi, *Zen Buddhism and the Reality of Suffering*,
https://doi.org/10.1007/978-3-031-69244-4_8

necessary to progress along the 'stages on the path'. Outside the main centres with their resident masters and teachers, much less is known about the role of meditation in smaller temples, and how or indeed whether meditation was practised at all by the local population of devotees. Some Asian reform movements, following Buddhist developments in the West, proposed renewed and simplified Zen and Vipassana meditation to make Buddhist practices more accessible.

The question of lay meditation outside temples has been examined in detail by Robert H. Sharf in his article *Buddhist Modernism and the Rhetoric of Meditative Experience* (Sharf, 1995). From this, it appears that the general lay population had limited experiential practice of meditation, and in the twentieth century, it became clear how challenging it would be for lay devotees to be integrated into traditional practices. This happened in South Asia for the Theravada tradition, when in Myanmar, the Theravada Buddhist monk Mahasi Sayadaw, whose *Mahasi School* had gained a significant foothold also in Sri Lanka, proposed a revival of the Vipassana practice. In particular, he focused on Vipassana meditation, strictly adhering to the tradition's moral rules and principles (Sayadaw, 1987).

In Japan, a similar situation arose, when attempts were made to make Zen Buddhism more accessible to the lay public. Shinichi Hisamatsu, a philosopher and Zen scholar, founded the *F.A.S. Society* in Kyoto in the early twentieth century and proposed a radically simplified version of Zen practice. He suggested to focus the practice on a single *fundamental koan*, using *mutual inquiry* within the group of students to replace *sanzen*, the traditional individual interview with the master (F.A.S. Society, 2022). Hakuun Yasutani also proposed a simplification in 1954, in the form of *Sanbo Kyodan*, a combination of Soto and Rinzai practices. This idea attracted a number of individuals who had played important roles in the diffusion of Zen in the West, such as Philip Kapleau, Robert Aitken and the Roman Catholic priest Hugo Enomiya-Lassalle. The movement gained some popularity and remains extant in the West today (Kapleau, 1989). Sharf goes as far as to suggest that in some cases, these efforts focused on supporting the interests of institutional legitimation (Sharf, 1995). Substantial efforts were thus realised to make Buddhist practice more accessible to lay modern society and were called *protestant* or *secular* by proponents like Stephen Batchelor (Batchelor, 2017).

From this base, at the end of the 1990s, the unexpected new Western *mindfulness* movement appeared and gained widespread popularity.

Before examining it in more detail, it is worth exploring the root of the term 'mindfulness'. It is generally accepted that T.W. Rhys Davids coined the term as an English translation of the Pali term *sati* and its Sanskrit synonym *smrti*. The translation was universally accepted in English-speaking communities, and presumably because of its simplicity and directness, the term was quickly adopted by other Western languages. *Sati* and *smrti* are specific terms originally used in Buddhism in relation to the cultivation of a healthy mind, and the term *sati* widely appeared in the Nikayas, the collections of the original Buddha's teachings, which are now accessible in English (Hwang & Kearny, 2015).

There is, however, an intricate and complex framework around the term *sati*, and mindfulness has therefore acquired a number of different meanings depending on its context. Indeed, the traditional Buddhist schools share adherence to the Noble Eightfold Path, which together with *wisdom* and *morality* requires the practice of *meditation*, through *right effort* together with *sati* and *samadhi*. The meaning of *sati* in this context is complex, and it implies a number of concepts ranging from the literal meaning of memory to something such as awareness, presence of mind and attentiveness to the moment; with this complex range of implications, the term is essential to the practice of Buddhism. Mindfulness as sati is definitely a constitutive part of the traditional practice of Zen Mahayana schools, and of the Hinayana Theravada tradition with its emphasis on the *Satipatthana Sutta*, with the *Four Establishments of Mindfulness* as well as the *Anapanasati Sutta* with its *Mindfulness of Breathing*. The Vipassana and the modernised Mahasi Sayadaw's movement are closely focused on the contents of these sutras and emphasise the role of sati as *bare attention*.

It is worth noting that *sati* is a constitutive element of Buddhist meditation together with *samadhi*, a state of deep concentration where *mindlessness*, an empty mind, is achieved, as recalled also in the Heart Sutra as *prajna paramita*. The relationship between these mind states poses additional challenges which have so far received little attention. The differences between samadhi-mindlessness and sati-mindfulness have been considered in some detail in Sharf's article *Mindfulness and Mindlessness in Early Chan* (Sharf, 2014).

Buddhist meditation continues to be followed in its traditional form in the various schools, involving the sati-mindfulness combined together with the mindlessness of *samadhi* and *shikantaza* of the Noble Eightfold Path. The fundamental importance of meditation is also stressed in the modern Mahasi's Vipassana movement and has a central role in the teachings of Thich Nhat Hanh. After completing his formal training in the Rinzai tradition, he promoted in both the East and the West what he called *engaged Buddhism*. He also established centres, named the Plum Villages, where his followers could live and practice the core teachings of Buddhism (Hạnh, 2019). Thich Nhat Hanh clearly and succinctly expressed the essence of Buddhist principles in many books. Along with formal commentaries on classic texts like the *Record of Master Linji* (Hạnh, 2007), he also insisted on the concept of mindfulness in a traditional way. In *Transformation and Healing*, for example, he delved into the *Sutra of the Four Establishments of Mindfulness*, which is also at the heart of Theravada and Vipassana principles (Hanh, 2006). At the same time, he produced an original approach to mindfulness, expressing the Buddha's Five Precepts in a modern and accessible form in his book, *Happiness, the Five Mindfulness Trainings* (Hạnh, 2016).

While Buddhism, with its mindfulness and mindlessness practices, was quietly taking hold in the West, something happened that would radically change the nature of meditation and its uses. At the end of the 1990s, Jon Kabat-Zinn devised the *Mindfulness-Based Stress Reduction* (MBSR) programme, and established the *Stress Reduction Clinic* at the University of Massachusetts Medical Centre.

On the basis of his personal experience with *Korean Seon Buddhism* and the *Insight Meditation Society* (IMS), Kabat-Zinn was convinced that patients, whose mental conditions had not so far been effectively treated with conventional medical interventions, could find relief in 'mindfulness meditation'. Given the secular context in which he operated, he decided to avoid any reference to the cultural, religious Buddhist origins of meditation and mindfulness and devised an eight-week intervention. It included *body scanning*, was supported by yoga and was originally based on guided sitting and walking meditation that was inspired by Buddhism but stripped of its context. The representative definition he provided for his mindfulness intervention was: 'the awareness that emerges through paying attention on purpose, in the present moment and nonjudgmentally, to the unfolding of experience moment by moment' (Kabat-Zinn, 2003, 2013). A key point here is that Kabat-Zinn's mindfulness-based intervention (MBI) was developed in the framework of conventional evidence-based medicine, in order to scientifically and objectively assess the results obtained. Kabat-Zinn immediately showed that his proposal was effective, and the first trial on patients with psoriasis (Kabat-Zinn et al., 1998) was rapidly followed by numerous experimental studies and clinical trials on a wide range of different conditions.

Kabat-Zinn has been extremely active and effective in promoting his mindfulness intervention and the MBSR. He has a highly enthusiastic follower base, and mindfulness has become so popular that it has moved beyond niche publications, even appearing on the cover of Time magazine in the issue *The Mindful Revolution* (The Mindful Revolution, 2014).

In subsequent decades, MBSR was quickly adopted by the cognitive neurosciences and cognitive behaviour therapies (CBT). New, third-wave approaches were created, such as *Mindfulness-Based Cognitive Therapy* (MBCT), *Acceptance and Commitment Therapy* (ACT) and *Dialectic Behaviour Therapy* (DBT) (Hwang & Kearny, 2015).

MBCT was proposed by a group of British and Canadian researchers as a combination of CBT with MBSR to treat depressive mood disorders (Segal et al., 2018). ACT also combines the principles of cognitive therapy and mindfulness in an approach mainly used to treat post-traumatic stress disorders (Hayes et al., 2016).

DBT is a structured, high-intensity approach that combines aspects of cognitive and mindfulness interventions. It is based on the synthesis and integration of opposites and aims to treat conditions like serious mood disorders with suicidal risks, borderline personality disorders, and substance abuse (Swenson, 2018; Linehan, 2014). DBT was developed by Marsha Linehan, who revealed that she herself had suffered from borderline personality disorder. She also had direct experience with the practice of Buddhism and Zen meditation, having received spiritual guidance and training in the USA from Gerald May and Tilden Edwards, as well as from Willigis Jaeger Roshi at the *Sanbo Kyodan School* in Germany. She then went on to become an associate Zen teacher at the *Diamond Sangha* in the USA (Marsha Linehan Biography, 2019; Linehan, 2021). More details about this are available in *What's Mindfulness?* in *Psychotherapy, Mindfulness and Buddhist Meditation* (Giraldi, 2020b).

Since 1970, the number of scientific papers on mindfulness and the effects of mindfulness-based interventions has grown enormously, along with an even greater number of news articles. In 2017, *Perspectives on Psychological Science* published an article called *Mind the Hype: A Critical Evaluation and Prescriptive Agenda for Research in Mindfulness and Meditation*, reporting that from 1970 to 2015, the number of scientific articles on mindfulness increased from zero to 1200, while the number of news articles exploded to 34,000 (Van Dam et al., 2017).

The number and range of monographs are similarly extensive. The titles of the Springer book series published from 2012 to 2024 are indicative: *Exploring Frontiers of the Mind-Brain Relationship*; *Mindful Parenting, New Directions in Research and Practice, Mindfulness Intervention for Children with Autism Spectrum Disorders*; *Buddhist Foundations of Mindfulness; Handbook of Mindfulness*; *Practitioner's Guide to Ethics and Mindfulness-Based Interventions; Handbook of Zen, Mindfulness, and Behavioral Health*; *Handbook of Ethical Foundations of Mindfulness*; *Mindfulness for Everyday Living. A Guide for Mental Health Practitioners; Handbook of Self-Compassion*; and *Mindfulness for Children, Adolescents, and Families: Integrating Research into Practice*.

This huge body of literature has made it possible to identify several critical issues, which have been explored in *Mind the Hype: A Critical Evaluation and Prescriptive Agenda for Research in Mindfulness and Meditation* (Van Dam et al., 2017) and *Methodological Flaws and the Evidence of Efficacy* (Giraldi, 2020a).

The first problem is the semantic meaning of mindfulness, which has already been considered above. Throughout the literature, it has been given a wide range of meanings, often without clear distinction between mindfulness, meditation and their combination as mindfulness meditation.

Most of the studies that attempt to evidence efficacy involve a small number of subjects and provide poorly reproducible results. The prevailing criteria for inclusion are the diagnostic categories from the American Psychiatric Association's *Diagnostic Statistic Manual.* In the majority of studies, they select subjects and assess results using psychometric questionnaires that detail criteria adhering to the principles of cognitive science and cognitive-behavioural interventions, adopted by biological psychiatry. This led Van Dam and his collaborators to argue that there was 'insufficient construct validity in measuring mindfulness', leading to a 'replication crisis' in the results reported. The poor methodological quality of the scientific evidence supporting these treatments has been evidenced, and there has been some modest adoption of the recommendations for improvement (Goldberg et al., 2018). Van Dam also considered the opportunity to investigate mindfulness through contemplative neuroscience (Van Dam et al., 2017), which may inspire researchers to avoid quantitative procedures and choose qualitative and narrative approaches.

After Kabat-Zinn's initial work, a large proportion of studies continue to use evidence-based clinical trials. The gold standard for these studies requires a 'double blind' placebo. Neither the subject receiving the treatment nor the therapist and the evaluator of the results should know whether the treatment received was a placebo. This problem has already come up when assessing the efficacy of psychotherapies and has been deemed almost impossible to overcome. The *Journal of Clinical Psychology* devoted a whole issue to the placebo phenomenon; it is easy to imagine the additional difficulties faced in evaluating the role of placebos in mindfulness studies (Herbert & Gaudiano, 2005).

In most countries where psychotherapeutic interventions are carried out, talking cure providers require formal training and certification. Given the large number of psychotherapies available, however, this can be a challenge. And when the range of often poorly defined mindfulness interventions is considered, the problem of proper qualification becomes even greater. For Kabat-Zinn's MBSR, a practitioner can become a qualified 'mindfulness instructor' after formal training. In the UK, it is also possible to gain MBCT-specific certification for meditation, in addition to CBT.

It is clear, however, that the training and competency of MBCT therapists is a challenge, and this has been considered in structured, controlled, randomised studies on mindfulness-based interventions. The solution adopted for cognitive-behavioural therapies is to use manuals to train and assess therapists, and similar procedures have been used for MBCT (Kuyken et al., 2015). Competence in meditation, however, has received little attention in the wider field of MBCT (Feldman et al., 2019), raising the issue of the 'quantity' and 'quality' of meditation in modern mindfulness interventions.

Additionally, many other psychotherapists also often include 'wild' procedures inspired by mindfulness in their therapy, without specific recognised training.

These and other issues arose during the spread of mindfulness in the West, particularly in the USA, of which Ronald Purser has been one of the most vocal critics. In 2019, he published in the British newspaper *The Guardian* an article called *The Mindfulness Conspiracy* where he argues that mindfulness 'is sold as a force that can help us cope with the ravages of capitalism' (Purser, 2019b). The issues he raises deserve careful consideration and are expressed in more detail in the book he published the same year called *McMindfulness: How Mindfulness Became the New Capitalist Spirituality* (Purser, 2019a). The engaging term *McMindfulness* was previously coined by Miles Neale, a Buddhist teacher and psychotherapist for 'a feeding frenzy of spiritual practices that provide immediate nutrition but no long-term sustenance: the contemporary fad for mindfulness is the entrepreneurial equal of McDonald's' (Purser, 2019b). For Purser, mindfulness has been oversold and commodified, and reduced to a technique for just any instrumental purpose. He is not alone in being concerned about the Western colonisation and commercialisation of Asian wisdom since the eighteenth century, and this is expressed by Jeremy Carrett and Richard King in their book *Selling Spirituality. The Silent Take over of Religion* (Carrette & King, 2011). Mindfulness is described as successfully integrated into modern globalised neoliberalism, where people are sold mindful approaches to parenting, eating, teaching, therapy, leadership, finance, nationhood, military resilience and dog ownership, to name just a few. Mindfulness is estimated to be a four-billion-dollar industry, including over 50,000 published books (Purser, 2019b). How mindfulness is marketed is explored in more detail by Jeff Wilson in his book *Mindful America: The Mutual Transformation of Buddhist Meditation and American Culture*, together with other relevant issues such as its medicalisation and relationship to moral values (Wilson, 2014). One particular feature of mindfulness as it has developed in the West is the sheer narcissism of its framing, which emphasises selfish values that are far removed from its Buddhist origins (Joiner, 2017).

Attempts have been made to build a connection between mindfulness and science, mainly neurosciences, and a new field has appeared: the science of meditation. A crucial inspiration for this was the dialogue between a group of American scientists and Tibetan Buddhism, particularly through the Dalai Lama. This produced a series of encounters, the *Mind and Life Dialogues*, whose results have been reported in books such as *The Science of Meditation: How to Change Your Brain, Mind and Body* (Goleman & Davidson, 2018b) and *Altered Traits: Science Reveals How Meditation Changes Your Mind, Brain, and Body* (Goleman & Davidson, 2018a).

In the following years, numerous investigations were made using the most advanced neuroscience techniques, such as brain imaging with functional magnetic resonance (fMRI) and even identifying the polymorphism of genetic factors that could be involved. Devices such as electroencephalographic (EEG) wearable sensors, together with computer programmes and a wide variety of mobile phone applications, were also developed, marketed and gained broad popularity.

Attempts have been made to trace the brain mechanisms behind the effects of meditation, and the results have been reviewed in *Nature Review Neuroscience*. The authors conclude that there is little doubt that various forms of meditation influence the functioning of the brain in many identifiable ways, but 'the underlying neural mechanisms remain unclear, and it is apparent that more methodologically rigorous studies are required if we are to gain a full understanding of the neuronal and molecular bases of the changes in the brain that accompany mindfulness meditation' (Tang, 2017).

In December 2021, *Nature* also published a portfolio of 16 articles called *Effects of Meditation and Mindfulness,* which aimed to bring together some of the latest research in the field. The subjects include the physiological, neural and psychological effects of these practices, as well as an amazingly varied range of other topics such as the activation of altruism; romantic relationship wellbeing; stress, emotion, spirituality and heart rate; brain structure and thoughtfulness and thoughtlessness; telomeres length; and other psychological and physical questions. The variety of topics is evident, as is the range of procedures: there is no precise distinction between meditation, mindfulness and mindfulness meditation. The MBSR protocol is mainly followed, together with a large variety of poorly defined modalities of different duration; in one case, the *sufi Tamarkoz* meditation was used. The subjects varied from young students to older individuals, but overall, they were prevailingly healthy adults, though in two instances, there were groups of patients with cardiac or bowel diseases. Their number varied from one subject to a larger sample which was followed longitudinally; their experience ranged from beginner novices to long-term meditators ('Editor's choice: the effects of meditation and mindfulness', 2021).

It is clear that meditation, following extremely different procedures, causes a wide range of psychological and somatic effects. Little is known and published about the trials that produced negative results or results that were deemed insufficient to warrant publication in peer-reviewed journals. Little thought seems to have been given to the possibility of adverse side effects, too (Farias & Wikholm, 2016).

Many studies continue to be performed and published; a PubMed search with the keyword 'mindfulness' shows more than 28,000 articles from 1970 to 2023, more than 3700 during 2023 alone. They provide interesting bits of information, when the problems of practical and clinical significance as well as reproducibility, are adequately addressed. However, when these studies have merited publication, the issue that still arises is that they cover a huge range of findings and lack coherent, general contextualisation.

Mindfulness-based interventions appear to face problems similar to those of psychology and psychotherapies, namely the dichotomy between a humanistic approach inaccessible to the investigation by *hard science*, and the neurosciences with their cognitive and behavioural therapies which are deemed to be reductively mechanistic.

Carl Gustav Jung's claim that 'the goal in psychotherapy is exactly the same as in Buddhism', clearly applies to his analytical psychology. It returns us to a possible commonality between person-oriented psychotherapies and Buddhism: both identify a reactive source for the existential ailments of life, and both suggest this can be relieved, either during analysis or by following the Noble Eightfold Path.

Cognitively oriented therapies, on the other hand, are confined in an empirical frame, which identifies the sufferings of life based on the distance between an individual and the average population, specified using diagnostic manual and psychometric questionnaires. The effects of the interventions are then quantitatively evaluated based on statistical significance.

Many criticisms have been raised against MBSR, MBCT and third-generation cognitive therapies based on these concerns, so many in fact as to allow a meta-analysis entitled *A Meta-Critique of Mindfulness; From McMindfulness to Critical Mindfulness* (Walsh, 'A meta-critique of mindfulness; from McMindfulness to critical mindfulness', 2016).

Horgan has also provided a more general contribution in this area, with his interviews of experts in scientific explorations of the mind, collected in *The Undiscovered Mind: How the Human Brain Defies Replication, Medication, and Explanation* (Horgan, 2000) and *Rational Mysticism: Dispatches from the Border Between Science and Spirituality* (Horgan, 2004). Through these, his basic pessimism about the future progress of science, including the science of the brain and mind, becomes clear, which he expressed directly in *The End of Science: Facing the Limits of Knowledge in the Twilight of the Scientific Age* (Horgan, 2015).

Wampold has also considered the factors that influence the results of psychotherapies, and which he believes have not received enough attention in other quarters. He found that the patient-therapist relationship depends on alliance, empathy and expectations and that positive matching between the individual characteristics of the patient and the therapist also plays a crucial role. Moreover, there are also large differences in the general competence and effectiveness of therapists.

An additional theme which has received marginal attention, if any, is the proliferation in the number of psychotherapies. Approximately five hundred different psychotherapies have been developed following Sigmund Freud's initial proposal of psychoanalysis as the talking cure for neurotic suffering.

In Wampold's work on the specific factors determining the success of psychotherapy, he focused mainly on the differences between treatments and much less on rated competence, adherence to the protocol and the *specific ingredients*. Even more revealing is that the contribution of the *specific ingredients*, the specific factors that should differentiate one psychotherapy from another, is extremely small and only marginally contributes to the success of the overall intervention (Wampold & Imel, 2015).

The implication for the proliferation of psychotherapies is evident. While there is sound evidence that they cause significant therapeutic effects, though of limited magnitude, no evidence has yet been found using the best procedures available, that one is better than another, independent of the theoretical background used to attempt to justify their differences.

It is possible to apply this view to mindfulness-based interventions. While MBCT has been shown to be effective in treating individuals at risk of depressive relapse or recurrence, no attempt appears to have been made to compare MBCT with CBT or, in other words, to show that the mindfulness component of MBCT is the *active ingredient*.

Mindfulness currently encompasses an archipelago of different uses and ideas, which span from the purest traditional Buddhist practices to the introduction of an increasing number of third-wave cognitive therapies that involve the use of meditation by therapists who are poorly experienced in its practice. The mindfulness interventions that are so popular now, and which many have attempted to embed in the evidence-based clinical procedures of psychology and psychiatry, will certainly continue to evolve in future. And Buddhism, too, will undoubtedly continue to change and adapt to the demands of a globalised world, integrating itself further into the West into which it has only so recently been introduced. As these changes occur, they will also certainly influence how we face the sufferings that unavoidably accompany the trajectory of life, and it will be fascinating to see how this will happen.

References

Batchelor, S. (2017). *Secular Buddhism*. Yale University Press.

Carrette, J. R., & King, R. (2011). *Selling spirituality: The Silent takeover of religion*. Routledge.

'Editor's choice: The effects of meditation and mindfulness'. (2021). *Nature news*. Retrieved February 13, 2024, from https://www.nature.com/collections/ibhachifaj

F.A.S. Society. (2022). *Introduction to FAS*. Retrieved January 26, 2024, from http://www.fas.x0.com/about/aboutuse.html

Farias, M., & Wikholm, C. (2016). Has the science of mindfulness lost its mind? *BJPsych Bulletin, 40*(6), 329–332. https://doi.org/10.1192/pb.bp.116.053686

Feldman, C., Kuyken, W., & Segal, Z. (2019). *Mindfulness: Ancient wisdom meets modern psychology*. The Guilford Press.

Giraldi, T. (2020a). Methodological flaws and the evidence of efficacy. In *Mindfulness, psychotherapy and Buddhist meditation* (pp. 143–188). Palgrave Macmillan.

Giraldi, T. (2020b). What's mindfulness. In *Psychotherapy, mindfulness and Buddhist meditation* (pp. 13–35). Palgrave Macmillan.

Goldberg, S., et al. (2018). *Is mindfulness research methodology improving over time? A systematic review* [Preprint]. https://doi.org/10.31231/osf.io/nm7a8

Goleman, D., & Davidson, R. J. (2018a). *Altered traits: Science reveals how meditation changes your mind, brain, and body*. Avery, an imprint of Penguin Random House LLC.

Goleman, D., & Davidson, R. J. (2018b). *The science of meditation: How to change your brain, mind and body*. Penguin Life.

Hanh, T. N. (2006). *Transformation and healing*. Parallax Press.

Hạnh, T. N. (2007). *Nothing to do, nowhere to go: Reflections on the teachings of Zen master Lin Chi*. Parallax.

Hạnh, T. N. (2016). The five mindfulness trainings. In *Happiness: Essential mindfulness practices* (pp. 35–38). Jaico Publishing House.

Hạnh, T. N. (2019). *At home in the World: Stories and essential teachings from a monk's life*. Parallax Press.

Hayes, S. C., Strosahl, K., & Wilson, K. G. (2016). *Acceptance and commitment therapy: The process and practice of Mindful Change*. The Guilford Press.

Herbert, J. D., & Gaudiano, B. A. (2005). Introduction to the special issue on the placebo concept in psychotherapy. *Journal of Clinical Psychology, 61*(7), 787–790. https://doi.org/10.1002/jclp.20125
Horgan, J. (2000). *The undiscovered mind: How the human brain defies replication, medication, and explanation*. Simon & Schuster.
Horgan, J. (2004). *Rational mysticism: Dispatches from the border between science and spirituality*. Houghton Mifflin.
Horgan, J. (2015). *The end of science: Facing the limits of knowledge in the twilight of the scientific age*. Basic Books.
Hwang, Y. S., & Kearny, P. (2015). A genealogy of mindfulness. In *A mindfulness intervention for children with autism spectrum disorder* (pp. 5–21). Springer.
Joiner, T. (2017). *Mindlessness: The corruption of mindfulness in a culture of narcissism*. Oxford University Press.
Kabat-Zinn, J. (2003). Mindfulness-based interventions in context: Past, present, and future. *Clinical Psychology: Science and Practice, 10*(2), 144–156. https://doi.org/10.1093/clipsy/bpg016
Kabat-Zinn, J. (2013). *Full catastrophe living: Using the wisdom of your body and mind to face stress, pain, and illness; the mindfulness-based stress reduction (MBSR) program used in medical centers worldwide*. Bantam Books.
Kabat-Zinn, J., et al. (1998). Influence of a mindfulness meditation-based stress reduction intervention on rates of skin clearing in patients with moderate to severe psoriasis undergoing photo therapy (UVB) and photochemotherapy (PUVA). *Psychosomatic Medicine, 60*(5), 625–632. https://doi.org/10.1097/00006842-199809000-00020
Kapleau, P. (1989). *The three pillars of Zen*. Doubleday.
Kuyken, W., et al. (2015). The effectiveness and cost-effectiveness of mindfulness-based cognitive therapy compared with maintenance antidepressant treatment in the prevention of depressive relapse/recurrence: Results of a randomised controlled trial (the prevent study). *Health Technology Assessment, 19*(73), 1–124. https://doi.org/10.3310/hta19730
Linehan, M. (2014). *DBT skills training: Handouts and worksheets*. Guilford Press.
Linehan, M. (2021). *Building a life worth living: A memoir*. Random House.
Marsha Linehan Biography. (2019). *Behavioral Research Therapy Clinics*. Retrieved February 2, 2024, from https://depts.washington.edu/uwbrtc/our-team/marsha-linehan/
Purser, R. E. (2019a). *McMindfulness: How mindfulness became the new capitalist spirituality*. Repeater.

Purser, R. E. (2019b). The mindfulness conspiracy. *The Guardian*. Retrieved February 9, 2024, from https://www.theguardian.com/lifeandstyle/2019/jun/14/the-mindfulness-conspiracy-capitalist-spirituality

Sayadaw, M. (1987). *Fundamentals of Vipassana meditation*. Kuala Lumpur.

Segal, Z. V., et al. (2018). *Mindfulness-based cognitive therapy for Depression*. The Guilford Press.

Sharf, R. (1995). Buddhist modernism and the rhetoric of meditative experience. *Numen, 42*(3), 228–283. https://doi.org/10.1163/1568527952598549

Sharf, R. (2014). Mindfulness and mindlessness in early chan. *Philosophy East and West, 64*(4), 933–964. https://doi.org/10.1353/pew.2014.0074

Swenson, C. R. (2018). *DBT principles in action: Acceptance, change, and Dialectics*. Guilford.

Tang, Y.-Y. (2017). Brain mechanisms of mindfulness meditation. In *The neuroscience of mindfulness meditation* (pp. 9–22). https://doi.org/10.1007/978-3-319-46322-3_2

'The Mindful Revolution'. (2014). *Time*. Retrieved February 2, 2024, from https://content.time.com/time/covers/0,16641,20140203,00.html

Van Dam, N. T., et al. (2017). Mind the hype: A critical evaluation and prescriptive agenda for research on mindfulness and meditation. *Perspectives on Psychological Science, 13*(1), 36–61. https://doi.org/10.1177/1745691617709589

Walsh, Z. (2016). A meta-critique of mindfulness; from McMindfulness to critical mindfulness. In *Handbook of mindfulness* (pp. 153–166). Springer.

Wampold, W. B. E., & Imel, Z. E. (2015). *The great psychotherapy debate: The evidence for what makes psychotherapy work*. Routledge, Taylor & Francis Group.

Wilson, J. (2014). *Mindful America: The mutual transformation of Buddhist meditation and American culture*. Oxford University Press.

9

Zen Meditation in an Open Public Mental Health Institution

This chapter will explore the work that has been done to incorporate the practice of zazen, Zen meditation, into an open public health institution in Trieste, Italy. The institution is now part of the University and National Health Services of Trieste campus for mental health and psychiatry. It is located in the renovated site of a psychiatric asylum, called *phrenocomion*, a sort of beautiful, independent village that was built by the Austrian empress Maria Theresia at the end of the eighteenth century, on a large green site on a hill at the edge of the city. The facilities were designed to provide the best comprehensive care available at those times to patients suffering from mental illnesses.

Until the eighteenth century, Trieste had been a small fishing village on the coast of the northern Adriatic, ruled by the Habsburg empire. It was, however, destined to have a unique role. Thanks to the foresight of the empress Maria Theresia, it grew in just a few decades to become a bustling port city, filled with growing shipyards, shipping, insurance companies and other commercial activities. As it grew, it also developed closer ties with the lively culture of the Austrian capital, Vienna. This included medical developments, and it was as part of this flourishing that the new, state-of-the-art psychiatric institution was constructed.

T. Giraldi, *Zen Buddhism and the Reality of Suffering*,
https://doi.org/10.1007/978-3-031-69244-4_9

The asylum in Trieste played a significant role in the development of psychiatry. It became the centre for the introduction of psychoanalysis to Italy, through a doctor working there called Edoardo Weiss, who was personally trained by Sigmund Freud and Paul Federn (Gandolfi, 2010). Moreover, this is also the place where in the 1970s, Franco Basaglia, took the position of director and, with his collaborators, developed and applied his innovative ideas for a new psychiatry. The main principles were deinstitutionalisation and the extension of mental health approaches to the whole territory, respecting the social rights of subjects with mental problems. His work was inspired by existentialist and phenomenological principles, as well as by the work of sociological and historical critics of traditional psychiatric approaches. The amazingly positive results led to the national bill which was approved by the Italian parliament in 1978, the *Legge 180*,which abolished closed mental hospitals in Italy (Foot, 2014; Mezzina, 2014).

The place is now a campus hosting the Department of Mental Health of the National Health System (NHS) together with the Department of Psychology of Trieste University. It is a place where people suffering from mental ailments can be cared for by professional staff who are directly involved in helping them. There, students are also trained for careers in care professions like social work, psychiatric nursing, clinical psychology and psychiatry, along with psycho-social volunteering. The Department of Mental Health there, with its practitioners and patients, thus seemed an appropriate place for a person-centred approach to tackle so-called 'minor' mental health problems that lie outside serious mental disorders that require specific psychiatric attention. It also seemed the ideal place to apply Buddhism's core principles about existential suffering: a place that was open to innovation while preserving the essential humanistic, interpersonal and psychodynamic principles.

A project was thus devised and initiated in 2014, which is still under way, based on meditation. Specifically, it offers zazen meditation to patients experiencing mental suffering, to help them develop new coping skills to face their existential problems and mental health issues. The project also targeted mental healthcare professionals, to enhance their understanding about the implications of Buddhist principles for the existential sufferings of life. One further aim was to offer an alternative form of meditation to popular 'mindfulness' approaches that had lost their connection to Buddhist principles.

The first initiative gave staff members the option to involve their patients. It began with a cycle of lectures illustrating the principles behind the project, accompanied by a series of meditation sessions. The basic meditation approach was to be followed weekly for eight weeks. The first meeting included the collection of informed consent and the administration of the psychometric scale *Patient Health Questionnaire* (PHQ9), *General Anxiety Disorder* (GAD7) and *Mindful Attention Awareness Scale* (MAAS). The participants also had to give written answers to open questions about how they were feeling, how they imagined the experience of meditation and what their expectations were. At the end of the eight weeks, answers to similar open questions were collected, and the psychometric scale was readministered.

For the meditation, they sat cross-legged, or in positions as close as possible to that, for 20 minutes, concentrating on the abdomen, exhaling and counting repeatedly from one to ten. There was an initial period with a *body scan*, a relaxation and body awareness exercise, including a period of meditation while still lying down. This was followed by three periods of sitting meditation, with five minutes of walking meditation in between. Meditation continued during the series of the eight movements of Ba Duan Jin (Introduction & History of Ba Duan Jin, 2020) which ended the session. The participants were encouraged to practice meditation daily during the week at their homes, and during daily activities, particularly while walking.

The first stage involved 30 patients of the NHS facility for the mental care of teenagers, who were selected and accepted to enter the programme. The subjects suffered from general anxiety syndrome, with individual secondary comorbid conditions and, in two cases, minor psychotic symptoms. Only five completed the eight-week period planned. But amazingly, their psychiatric evaluation at the end of the intervention revealed a marked improvement, with a total disappearance, or a marked attenuation, of all or a large part of the symptoms; these subjects decided they did not need to continue their previous treatment.

The staff considered these results very positive and encouraged the continuation of the programme. At the same time, however, there were some obvious limitations.

The limited size of the group of participants, which also decreased before the completion of the planned intervention, means that meaningful quantitative analysis of the initial and final scores is not possible. However, the psychometric scales continued to be administered in the following interventions before together with the open questions, since it was considered useful for bringing subjects' attention to the areas and issues which they may not otherwise have considered.

The answers to the initial and final open questions are quite evocative. Practically all of the responses suggested a markedly positive experience with various individual nuances. They are clearly anecdotal and can be meaningfully reported in a narrative way. The text of the answers could also be subjected to a collective qualitative analysis (Alasuutari, 2010), which has not been performed so far and is planned for the future.

One further point that merits investigation is the question of why a large proportion of subjects abandoned the programme before completing it. Attempts were made to get explanations from those who quit, but only a small proportion gave answers, and these are so heterogeneous that it was impossible to identify any common, meaningful thread.

A second finding is that the suggestion to continue meditating at home or outside while walking was reportedly poorly followed, even when the experience during the planned intervention appeared positive.

These considerations have to be applied to the experiences reported below as well. Two courses were organised in 2017 and 2018 at the University of Trieste, to offer interested caregivers a theoretical and practical experience of meditation. The residential courses were entitled *Training for Mindfulness Meditation*, lasted a long weekend, and were held in a hut owned by the university in the regional Alps; a certificate of participation was given by the University to the attendees. The reported written experiences were again largely positive; the courses could not be repeated because of the limited number of entries, despite significant interest from aspiring participants, presumably because of the small size of the region.

Stress and burnout conditions also appeared to respond positively to the intervention when it was offered in 2017 and 2018 to groups of nurses involved in the domiciliary care of NHS patients with various conditions. The participants again reported a highly positive experience in subjective as well as professional terms.

Family members of subjects with Alzheimer's disease and related conditions can also experience similar stress and burnout. A specific group was organised in 2019 for caregivers cared for by the NHS. In 2019, the NHS sent another small group of patients who had been diagnosed with functional disorders, an atypical condition for which the neurological and psychiatric treatments had been found to be unsatisfactory (Barsky, 1999). The subjects tried meditation and had highly positive experiences, and some continued for a while after completing the programme.

In 2022, a continuous operation was set up in a nearby mental health centre (locally called the *Maddalena*) run by the Department of Mental Health. The progressively positive impact made it beneficial to keep the group open without any scheduled structure, so people could enter it and continue irregularly; sitting meditation was limited to one period. Participation was extremely varied and included subjects whose conditions ranged from existential problems to serious psychiatric disorders for which they were receiving pharmacotherapy with antipsychotic drugs. The staff judged the impact on participants positively, and they encouraged its continuation and suggested it to other participants. To our surprise, it was particularly the psychiatric patients with psychotic syndromes for which they were receiving pharmacotherapy, who enjoyed the experience of meditation, regularly continued for long periods, and followed the recommendation to include meditation while walking and during their daily activities.

Zen meditation was also proposed in a completely different context, to the students of the University of Trieste. The regional authority responsible for the support of higher education (ARDIS), together with the University of Trieste, is concerned for the wellbeing of students and have organised services to provide psychological support. They therefore accepted the proposal to organise an experiential course on meditation. This was announced on the university website and social media as a *non-course on mindlessness*, for underlining its differences from just a series of frontal lectures and from the current mindfulness approaches. To everybody's surprise, there was a high number of entries in 2022, so numbers had to be limited to 30, which was the maximum practically acceptable. The experience was repeated twice in 2023 and continues in 2024, with the number of participants increased to 60, with a waiting list of over 100. The structure for meetings is a short lecture on the basic context of Buddhism, followed by Zen meditation. The local musical conservatory has been inspired by the experience and is planning to include its students in this offer of meditation, especially in relation to the anxiety and distress that can arise during public performances.

These experiences have been possible because of the author's background in mental health and psychotherapy, as well as Zen practice and meditation. They have been organised in collaboration with the *Association of Volunteering Franco Basaglia* (AVFB), which is based in the university campus where the management of the Department of Mental Health (DSM, Dipartimento di Salute Mentale) and the Faculty of Psychology are located. AVFB contributes to the local mental care provided by the DSM and to the postgraduate training of psychology students. Meditation sessions were initially carried out in its main hall and later also in the Centre for Mental Health of Maddalena and in one of the University of Trieste student houses. An additional facility available is the *Chudo*, the zendo of The Middle Way association, a place for Zen practice and meditation integrated into the national network of Buddhist Rinzai Zen centres, where the practice may continue after the initial stages described above.

Complex results have been collected over the last ten years of practice. The number of participants beginning and completing the initiatives is limited, and this necessarily limits any description to the anecdotal and narrative; a future qualitative analysis might provide additional information.

Overall, however, the experience definitely seemed positive for those who completed the proposed cycle, even if they did not formally continue their meditative practice at home or by joining *Chudo* association. Interest among professionals at the DSM service was high, and many encouraged their patients to try meditation for their existential mental ailments. However, they showed only limited interest in practicing meditation themselves, for their stress and burnout, even though this had previously been found to be helpful. They explained that their highly demanding and distressing job paradoxically prevented them from taking up any further burden.

The overall conclusions which can be drawn are that a relatively small proportion of subjects finished the planned intervention, and little or nothing could be understood from those abandoning the meditation programme. At the same time, there continue to be many requests to join Zen meditation groups, and the general evaluation of participants and external observers is positive.

The difficulty of describing the experience of Zen meditation in any way other than narrative or anecdotal forms constitutes a limitation to any attempts to report on this in a scientific, objective frame. At the same time, it can be noted that trying to make an average description or a quantitative evaluation of experiences which are so varied may be futile. The consideration of those who enjoyed it separately from those who did not complete it, or were not available for a follow-up, may be a more sensible approach, providing a moment of reflection for future interventions.

On the other hand, subjects may individually choose meditation and the humanistic perspective of Buddhism especially for more 'minor' mental disorders of an existential, reactive nature. This may avoid the alleged mechanistic reductionism of current psychiatric and cognitive behavioural psychotherapies and offer a more humanistic, person-centred, psychodynamic approach. The offer of meditation may thus fit effectively into the innovative mental health approaches initially developed in Trieste, in the perspective of respect for the individuality of patients while delivering the best psycho-social recovery they may attain.

References

Alasuutari, P. (2010). The rise and relevance of qualitative research. *International Journal of Social Research Methodology, 13*(2), 139–155. https://doi.org/10.1080/13645570902966056

Barsky, A. J. (1999). Functional somatic syndromes. *Annals of Internal Medicine, 130*(11), 910. https://doi.org/10.7326/0003-4819-130-11-199906010-00016

Foot, J. (2014). Franco Basaglia and the radical psychiatry movement in Italy, 1961–78. *Critical and Radical Social Work, 2*(2), 235–249. https://doi.org/10.1332/204986014x14002292074708

Gandolfi, L. (2010). Freud in Trieste: Journey to an ambiguous city. *Psychoanalysis and History, 12*(2), 129–151. https://doi.org/10.3366/pah.2010.0002

Introduction & History of Ba Duan Jin. (2020). *YouTube*. Retrieved March 7, 2024, from https://www.youtube.com/watch?v=poxClwHOLgs&list=PLLwoNfHmTuN6Adkh7H7oiXsz1QnyYHOnm&ab_channel=ChineseHealthQigongAssociation

Mezzina, R. (2014). Community mental health care in Trieste and beyond. *Journal of Nervous & Mental Disease, 202*(6), 440–445. https://doi.org/10.1097/nmd.0000000000000142

10

Epilogue

This book has examined Buddhism and Zen in relation to existential suffering, employing the simplest and most naturalistic approach possible for this complex subject. Its aim is also to sit alongside the many extant traditions, practices and writings that provide the mystic, spiritual, religious, philosophical and psychological framework for this area. The motivation behind this is to attempt to trace the central thread of the historic Buddha's teachings on meditation and its relationship to life suffering, and how this has developed in the centuries.

The task is challenging, given the huge amount of literature, for academic, expert and lay audiences. An essential starting point was provided by the unique and pioneering work of Daisetz Teitaro Suzuki, who translated the most relevant classical Zen texts into English, for Western readers (Haar et al., 1986).

Another key source was Christmas Humphreys and the Buddhist Society he founded in 1924 in London, and which he presided over until his death in 1983 (Humphreys, 2015). The Buddhist Society's work continues to this day and has proved to be extremely valuable for its interdenominational engagement, as a meeting point for the Zen, Theravada and Tibetan Vajrayana Buddhist traditions.

T. Giraldi, *Zen Buddhism and the Reality of Suffering*,
https://doi.org/10.1007/978-3-031-69244-4_10

Humphreys' *A Buddhist Student Manual* offers a basic, succinct guide to the rich body of Buddhist teachings (Humphreys, 1956). Another extremely concise, precise and effective guide, which unfortunately has not been translated from Italian, is *Il Buddhismo* and was written together with other valuable contributions by Giangiorgio Pasqualotto, Emeritus Professor of Philosophy at the University of Padova (Pasqualotto, 2003).

The foundations of Buddhism are considered unique in the history of human thought and religions. Siddhartha Gautama did not preach one all-powerful creator-judge as in the monotheistic religions, nor any revelation or sacred texts. His admonition to the Kalamas can be held as a good starting point here. His answer to questions about facing life's distressing events was not to rely on what has been acquired by repeated hearing, tradition, scriptures, axioms, specious reasoning, notions based on another's seeming ability, nor upon considering a monk as a teacher. His exhortation was for us to experience by ourselves: 'These things are good; these things are praised by the wise; undertaken and observed, these things lead to benefit and happiness, and to enter on and abide in them' (Soma, 2010). Following this advice, this book has attempted to avoid recourse to complex reasoning and argumentation, and this epilogue will continue in the same vein, to attempt to explore the central themes of reality and the sufferings which unavoidably accompany the trajectory of a life.

Following the Kalama admonition, the Four Noble Truths and the Noble Eightfold Path offer a clear beginning. Life's sufferings are caused by craving, desire and attachment, from which one can attempt to free oneself, by following the Eightfold Noble Path, the Middle Way.

These teachings are particularly relevant today, since they bring us towards psychology. Carl Gustav Jung argued that 'The goal in psychotherapy is exactly the same as in Buddhism', a statement that has to be seen as referring to analytical psychology, his field of expertise. The aim of the analytical process is to treat patients' neurotic suffering, attributed to real or imaginary previous traumas in their life, and which are hidden in their subconscious and are voluntarily inaccessible. In this approach, individual existential sufferings are conceived as being reactive, and practitioners focus their psychodynamic treatment on the elements that were initially responsible. These are the basic principles and starting point for many later psychotherapies and, alongside their psychodynamic nature, they can be seen as working from a broadly humanistic framework.

In Buddhism, a key concept close to the Four Noble Truths is that of the Three Marks of Existence, in which life's sufferings are related to the impermanence of reality, and the illusory nature of the individual self.

This brings us to a crucial difference between Buddhism and psychology, whose foundations and interventions are based on the principle of the existence and identification of the individual self. The existential sufferings are seen as challenges that arise from the involvement of the self in coping with life events; the goal of psychotherapy then is to help patients to develop more adaptive coping strategies.

It is worth noting that when psychoanalysis was developed, it was not conceived of a process working, in a clearly defined time, towards a specific therapeutic benefit: the analytic process was considered a path of personal growth. On the other hand, some psychotherapies developed in the second half of the twentieth century were based on completely different behavioural and cognitive principles, diverging significantly from those of the psychodynamic approaches. They were developed in an empirical form, without a conceptual foundation that could account for the identification of life's sufferings in an existential, humanistic framework. The therapists involved also lacked the extensive personal, experiential training required for psychotherapies based on psychodynamic principles. In these practices, the complexity of human thought, emotion and behaviour is reduced to an approach largely based on the use of psychometric questionnaires for the evaluation of patients, and manuals to train and assess therapists. It is for this reason that psychotherapies based on cognitive and behavioural principles have been accused of mechanistic reductionism.

The whole structure of Buddhism brings unavoidably to the question of how the ordinary mind can be awakened to enlightenment. This comes across clearly in the Bodhisattva Vows, which characterise the road to enlightenment as altruistic, requiring the shedding of attachments. Altruism is central to Mahayana Buddhism, and it concerns the morality and wisdom that arise with meditation as one follows the Middle Way.

According to traditional Zen practice, it was clear that we do not have direct access to our internal and external world. It is possible however to directly experience internal and external reality, without the filter of the thoughts and experiences accumulated in the self, and this can be attained with *kensho* and *satori*, through sitting meditation, zazen.

There is a huge body of classical and contemporary literature on *kensho, satori, koans* and enlightenment, which is largely rhetorical and self-referential and does not provide definite answers to the crucial questions involved. Some issues still remain unanswered: is there a real, definite experience of enlightenment, is it realized suddenly or gradually, and can its occurrence be distinguished with certainty. Additionally, is there any special yet natural state of consciousness, different from the ordinary mind, which might be objectively and scientifically identifiable.

Some answers to these questions have been offered by Ruth Fuller Sasaki, a Westerner with a deep, direct experience of Rinzai Zen, acquired during long sojourns in Daitokuji in Kyoto, which led her to be accepted as a fully certified Zen master, with her own recognised temple. Asked if a Western student could, after two or three years of practice in a Japanese temple, go home as an enlightened man, she said it was difficult to answer. She also added that even if he will have passed his first koan and he expects to have become what at present he conceived an enlightened man to be, then the answer is 'No', although the man who returns will be a different man from the one who came (Stirling & Snyder, 2006).

Scientific attempts to explore meditation and enlightenment have provided no clear answers, although it has been possible to gain clear evidence against individual identification with a self. Modern studies are fully in agreement with the basic Buddhist tenet that the self with which people identify has no physically identifiable nature and can be seen as a product of the functioning of the individual mind. This view is supported by a large body of evidence from neurology, neuropsychology and neurotoxicology, showing that a disruption of even a small part of the brain structure or function may lead to dramatic effects on the whole person, whose identity may be severely affected or even disrupted.

A great number of research results illustrate the attempts to explain meditation and have shown that it induces detectable changes in the functioning of the nervous system. Many of the studies use modern neuroscience techniques, such as fMRI of the brain in action, and even genomic studies on gene expression and epigenetics. These studies have in many cases produced sophisticated evidence about specific occurrences. The investigations, however, show isolated phenomena of limited extension and do not provide a definite evaluation of the magnitude and relevance of the findings to all the issues considered. Additionally, serious methodological problems have been evidenced, such as the small size of the samples and the poor reproducibility of the results, in addition to the criticised criteria used to define the researched area, as well as the subjects considered.

Similar difficulties have arisen with the enormous number of articles that have appeared in the literature since the 1970s, reporting results from modern Western mindfulness applied to stress and mood-related disorders.

Mindfulness certainly deserves adequate consideration because of its wide popularity and diffusion in the last couple of decades. The term itself is a translation of the Pali term *sati* or *smrti* in Sanskrit. Seen in this way, every Buddhist proceeding along the Middle Way practices mindfulness when they are engaged in meditation, together with the Right Effort and absorption in the deep state of *samadhi* meditation as described in the Middle Way.

In modern times, one key voice on mindfulness is Thich Nhat Hahn, the Vietnamese Zen Master who wrote extensively on the subject while perfectly adhering to Zen and Buddhist principles. He has preserved the traditional view of mindfulness in the practices of his Plum Villages, also in relation to the Five Precepts of Buddhism.

The modern interpretation of mindfulness, based on Buddhist meditation but stripped of its relations to Buddhism, arose in the 1990s through the work of Jon Kabat-Zinn. This interpretation focuses on non-judgemental awareness of the present. Zinn's initial Mindfulness-Based Stress Reduction (MBSR) programme aimed to reduce the negative consequences of stress in a Western medical context. His use of the term mindfulness proved fortunate, and soon, it was adopted in many different languages, possibly contributing to widespread popularity among professionals and the wider population.

The initial decision to identify meditation with sati-mindfulness is somewhat peculiar, however. Considering that the aim of all Buddhism is the cessation of life's sufferings, why, out of all the rich array of practices and teachings, just sati (translated as mindfulness) was chosen for meditation? This decision seems all the more perplexing given the fact that in all the Buddhist traditional schools, meditation is never stripped out of its wider context and the other principles that surround it. This is as clear for Zen, as it is in Hinayana Vipassana meditation, which is often cited by modern mindfulness followers. Moreover, the choice of one single aspect of meditation would seem more meaningful, if it would have been based on the universal Buddhist practice of the deep meditative state of the *prajna paramita*, *zazen*, *samadhi* and *shikantaza*.

Mindfulness, formally crystallised in Kabat-Zinn's MBSR intervention, is applied for a variety of medical conditions alongside stress reduction, particularly mood disorders like depression. Mindfulness has also been incorporated into cognitive psychotherapy, as *Mindfulness-Based Cognitive Therapy* (MBCT), as well as in other third-wave cognitive therapies such as *Dialectic Behavioural Therapy*. Many psychotherapists also include wildly some elements of mindfulness and meditation in their clinical practice, adding to the general problem of the practitioners' experience and qualification.

Evidence-based medicine has extensively examined mindfulness, in particular MBSR and MBCT, and the difficulties that have arisen have only added to those encountered in attempting to scientifically assess the results from cognitive and behavioural psychotherapies. The general methodological problems are the small sample sizes and ensuing limited reproducibility. Larger studies have been conducted with randomisation of subjects, but the main requirement for a proper *gold standard* trial, the inclusion of a double-blind placebo group, was not met and is likely impossible in this type of research. An additional critical issue is the criteria used to select subjects and evaluate the results. A large proportion of the studies on mindfulness characterise their patients using the diagnostic criteria of the American Psychiatric Association's *Diagnostic Statistics Manual* (DSM). As an example, the old terms of *melancholic endogenous depression* have been replaced with the DSM's *major depressive disorder*, and the effects of the intervention are evaluated using psychometric questionnaires of a similar nature. The complex human nature of existential sufferings is thus forced into a rigid, reductive framework, which has been met with substantial criticism. Studies based on the DSM diagnostic criteria may be inadequate for adequately evaluating the human characteristics of the subjects. Individuals who are perfectly mentally healthy and display mood changes that naturally result from coping with challenging life events cannot be distinguished from those with a morbid condition and can be formally diagnosed as having a mental disorder.

Even in best-planned research, another methodological issue arises when trying to report the positive effects of mindfulness-based interventions on mood disorders. MBCT was reported to be effective for depressive conditions that had responded poorly to previous treatments, while there was no direct comparison of MBCT with the *Cognitive Behavioural Therapy* (CBT) from which it originates. These studies do not therefore provide any evidence that the addition of mindfulness to CBT improves its effectiveness. This is a general problem with psychotherapies, humanistic or cognitively and behaviourally oriented, where the search for the *active ingredient* has shown its marginal relevance, and that the most important factor for their success is a positive human relationship between the patient and the therapist. It is worth noting that some current studies try to avoid the rigidity of evidence-based protocols and rely on humanistic methods. Narrative approaches have been used, and efforts are being made to replace the use of quantitative techniques with more adequate qualitative ones.

These are some of the developments and challenges in the last 30 years of mindfulness, and it will be interesting to see how it develops in future. It will also be interesting to see how Buddhism will integrate into Western cultures and whether and how it can provide answers to the challenges of coping with an increasingly globalised world.

These issues have to be considered in the context of the extraordinarily long life of Buddhism, with all the adaptations it has seen as it spread through Northern India, China and Tibet, as well as South East Asia and Japan. It was only recently that it reached the West, and when looking at its diffusion here, the deeply rooted anthropological characteristics that differentiate modern Western culture from the Eastern cultures where Buddhism developed have to be taken into account.

Zen is a prime example here, since its representation in Western literature and practice is so markedly different from the Japanese historic reality. In Japan, there has been for centuries throughout the country a wide network of temples and shrines, large and small, with their resident monks and masters. These structures provided services for the spiritual and religious needs of the population, the deeply rooted human needs that arose there, as they do in every culture and community. These needs were met by the temples and clergy, who satisfied the demand for rites such as funerals, marriages and other occurrences.

The contemporary diffusion of Buddhism in the West, on the other hand, is occurring in a largely Christian context, where emphasis on individuality and rational control of the human mind and natural world sharply contrasts with basic Eastern values. In Asia, the religiosity of the population was mainly expressed by adherence to Buddhist principles of morality and wisdom as well as the observance of the precepts: meditation was not practiced by the general lay population. Meditation is and has been a core practice in Zen temples for the training of priests, where monastic life is organised in a tight schedule. Some of the residing monks spend their entire life there as bachelors, taking decades to perfect and complete their training as masters, in order to continue the lineage of their master and temple. The challenges faced by laypeople in attempting to practice meditation have led to efforts to simplify Zen practice, such as those of the *F.A.S. Society* and *SamboKyodan*, which seem to have met with only limited success.

When Zen moved West, in North America and later Europe, it had to adapt to a radically different culture. The basic religious foundations there were Christian, Catholic and Protestant, with their emphasis on the value of the individual and on the rational mind, and included the faith and the scriptures, with their concept of sin, which is extraneous to the Eastern world, and even more so to Buddhism.

Zen initially laid roots in the West through the presence of Japanese masters in America, and new lineages of masters were soon established, with the authority to pass the Dharma on to their Western disciples, who established their new temples. Practices changed while they adapted to their new context, and sitting meditation acquired a central position, while the Buddhist principles of morality and wisdom, however, received less consideration.

Japan, as well as other Eastern Buddhist countries, is now facing new social developments that are markedly changing the relationship between the population and traditional Zen culture. A secularisation of younger generations is apparent, along with a growing distance from established values and traditions. New Buddhist movements, such as the *Soka Gakkai*, have been founded, aiming to reduce the distance between the population and the practice of Buddhism, seemingly with notable secular success.

These are some of the problems that Buddhism has to face in order to adapt to the third millennium with its rapid and pervasive changes. At the same time, new challenges arise for its integration into Western culture and society, as already noted for Zen by Christmas Humphreys in the 1960s (Humphreys, 1999).

Buddhism's core values have maintained their crystalline clarity, together with their richness and complexity, and remain actual despite the time that has passed since their beginnings. They give a unique representation of the human mind and the challenge of awakening the ordinary mind to the emptiness, selflessness and mindlessness of enlightenment, a puzzle and a tantalising goal. It will therefore be extremely interesting to see how Buddhism will once again succeed in adapting and yet staying true to its essential principles through the changing modern world, continuing to provide its message to humankind.

References

Haar, F., Abe, M., & Suzuki, D. T. (1986). *A Zen life: D.T. Suzuki remembered.* Weatherhill.

Humphreys, C. (1956). *A Buddhist students' manual.* Buddhist Society.

Humphreys, C. (1999). *A Western approach to Zen.* Quest Books.

Humphreys, C. (2015). *Both sides of the circle: The autobiography of Christmas Humphreys.* Routledge.

Pasqualotto, G. (2003). *Il Buddhismo. I sentieri di una religione millenaria.* Bruno Mondadori.

Soma, T. (2010). Kalama Sutta: The Buddha's charter of free inquiry. *Access to Insight* [Preprint]. Retrieved from http://www.accesstoinsight.org/lib/authors/soma/wheel008.html

Stirling, I., & Snyder, G. (2006). *Zen Pioneer: The Life & Works of Ruth Fuller Sasaki*. Shoemaker & Hoard.

Index[1]

[1] Note: Page numbers followed by 'n' refer to notes.

T. Giraldi, *Zen Buddhism and the Reality of Suffering*,
https://doi.org/10.1007/978-3-031-69244-4